Praise for *What kin*

"How often has one wondered wher
come from? There's no need to wonder an
a gem of a book that clearly and easily ...opean surnames and learn their meanings as well as accompanying historical traditions. Be careful though. Once you begin your first search, you'll be hooked and hungry for your next. *What Kind of Name is That?* is a pleasure of a compilation of history within families, links within life and relatives, and wonderment of the scatter-pattern of our world."

—Joan Fleiss Kaplan
Author of Set 6 story books in the Primary Phonics reading series
Co-author of *Buzz, Ruby, and Their City Chicks*

"Alma Barozzi analyzes the heritage of European surnames and identifies the naming patterns found in different European cultures. What kind of name is that? allows readers to peer into the past through surnames themselves and unlock the derivations and sources of these names, in many cases long obscured or forgotten. Her study is well-documented and imminently readable, making it enjoyable and informative for the seasoned linguist and the lay reader alike. Dr. Barozzi's linguistic curiosity and thorough scholarship inform her work. I highly recommend What kind of name is that? to anyone who has ever wondered where surnames come from and what they mean."

—Mary F. Richards
PhD, Slavic Languages and Literatures
Instructor in Latin and Russian

"Whether you are an expert at onomastics—the study of the etymology, history, and use of proper names—or never before heard the word, W*hat kind of name is that?* will offer you hours of intriguing information and entertainment. In this age when tracing one's ancestry is more compelling than studying a country's history, learning about the roots of your name seems a logical next step in the search for one's past."

— Judith Klein
MEd, Counseling
Communications and Marketing Specialist

Alma Barozzi has written a delightful, well researched and instructive book of relevance to all who have a curious mind. In this compelling discussion of European surnames, the author also delves into the ways last names reflect cultural norms, family structure and women's roles. I personally was fascinated by the variety of choices provided to women to choose a last name upon marriage and by the manner of assigning last names to illegitimate and orphaned children.

As an added bonus, What Kind of Name is That? offers important etiquette lessons for addressing those we interact with in the global economy. I truly look forward to Ms. Barozzi's next book on Asian surname traditions and hope she is planning on writing many additional books on the topic."

—Beth Saltzman Aaronson
Attorney and legal writing instructor

"Does your surname mean "clay marble baker", "wise one" or "rooster"? Or maybe it's derived from the blackberry grove near your ancestor's home, or harkens back to their curly hair. Finally, a factual, often humorous account of the European surnames we know so well. Sure to enlighten and entertain, W*hat kind of name is that?* is perfect for light reading or as a resource."

— Kali Reynolds
Education therapist
Executive function coach

What kind of name is that?

European Surnames: Meanings and Traditions

ALMA BAROZZI

What kind of name is that? European Surnames: Meanings and Traditions

Lilah Press
Boston, MA

For information contact: almabarozzi@yahoo.com

Book design by Steve Gladstone

ISBN: 979-8-9865832-04

NAMES

"Names, once they are in common use, quickly become mere sounds, their etymology being buried, like so many of the earth's marvels, beneath the dust of habit."

— Salman Rushdie

"A good name is rather to be chosen than riches."

— King Solomon

"Our names are labels, plainly printed on the bottled essence of our past behavior."

— Logan Pearsall Smith

“Names are not always what they seem.”

— Mark Twain

“I would rather make my name than inherit it.”

— William M. Thackeray

I dedicate this book to you, the Reader.
Whether you are here for professional or personal reasons—
for love of language as is manifest in the sounds and meanings of
names, for your interest in the field of genealogy, or out of
personal curiosity about your own heritage—this book is for you.
I hope you find what you're looking for and much more.

CONTENTS

List of Tables

List of Abbreviations

LG	Low German
MHG	Middle High German
OHG	Old High German
ME	Middle English (also known as Anglo-Norman or French Norman)
OE	Old English (also known as Anglo-Saxon)
OF	Old French
OW	Old Welsh
ON	Old Norse (in Scandinavian countries)
S	Serbian
C	Croatian
Sv	Slovene
B	Bosnian
M	masculine form
F	feminine form

All maps were created at https://www.mapchart.net/europe.html

Introduction

For as long as I can recall, I've been drawn to the diversity and mysterious origins of family names. Where are you from? Where is your family from? Your grandparents? Your roots? I asked these questions with curiosity and some trepidation, not wanting to make anyone feel uncomfortable. My kids would often point out to me the folly of such questions. They were politically incorrect; the people might feel offended, even afraid. I understood that. After a while, I learned that if I prefaced my questions with some specific facts about my own foreign background, the target of my curiosity would be more likely to respond.

Over the years, my interest expanded to the bearers of any unusual last name, whether I knew them or not, in front of me or on TV. I was fascinated by surname patterns in different cultures and I often searched for sources that might nurture my curiosity. There were plenty of books and articles on surnames specific to certain countries, but what I really wanted was an atlas of surnames. So I decided to create one.

Aside from satisfying our curiosity, a better understanding of surname traditions in different cultures can help us all become more culturally literate and avoid committing social gaffes. It wasn't that long ago that I heard a politician refer to the president of Mexico, Andrés Manuel López Obrador, as President Obrador, not understanding the meaning behind the double-barrelled surnames in Spanish-speaking countries. Some years ago I heard of an Icelandic couple who was visiting the US. After the woman introduced herself as, let's say, Anna Gísladóttir, someone turned to her husband saying "Nice to meet you, Mr. Gísladóttir." That person was unaware that a name ending in *-dóttir* could only belong to a woman and assumed that American naming patterns were universal. And if you're traveling through Hungary and you meet a man named Fodor Miklos, don't call him Fodor or Mr. Miklos. Hungarians tend to use the Eastern name order (family name followed by personal name). The information in this book should help us become more knowledgeable and aware of the great diversity in naming patterns in cultures other than our own.

The study of the history, origins, distribution and variations of names is called onomastics. As a field within linguistics, it can be anthroponymic (studying proper names of people) or toponymic (relating to place names).

Research in the field of anthroponymy can be of interest to researchers in many disciplines within social sciences, such as anthropology, sociology, history, geography, and genealogy, which has recently become a widespread field of research. The increasing availability of online resources and the latest advances in DNA research have generated huge interest in genealogical research not only by professional genealogists, but also by anyone who wishes to learn more about their family's history.

I started my research with European family names, as these were also the origins of most surnames in the New World. My first dilemma was the order and organization of the data I was about to amass. Should I organize it geographically, linguistically or culturally? Which order would offer the most natural transition from one group to the next? I was aware that naming patterns did not correspond neatly to nationalities or languages, that migration patterns, changing national borders, ethnic identities, and other factors affected naming customs and often blurred geographic boundaries. So I decided to use geographic location and language families as my primary variables while taking into account the history, nationality, ethnicity, and cultural mores that could have influenced naming practices over the centuries.

The second decision I had to make was which countries to include in my research. I decided to leave out Turkey and the Caucasus nations of Georgia, Armenia, and Azerbaijan, four countries located in the transition zone of Eastern Europe and Western Asia. The geographic boundaries between the two continents are typically considered to be the Ural Mountains, the Ural River, the Caspian Sea, the Caucasus Mountains and the Black Sea, connected to the Aegean Sea by the Strait of Bosporus, the Sea of Marmara and the Dardanelles. However, there is a lot more to the division of Eurasia than geographic lines. There are cultural, linguistic and ethnic differences which, when it comes to surname customs, are more important to consider. Therefore, Turkish, Georgian, Armenian and Azerbaijani surnames will be addressed in a separate study of Asian surname traditions.

Our voyage begins in southern Europe with Italy and moves clockwise, first west and north through Western Europe, then from the British Isles eastward through Scandinavia, the Baltic States, and finally southward through Eastern Europe and the Balkan Peninsula. It begins and ends on the shores of the Mediterranean and it makes stops in countries whose peoples speak a variety of mostly Indo-European languages (Romance, Germanic, Slavic, Greek) sprinkled with several non-Indo-European tongues. I hope you will find this journey as fascinating as I have.

SOUTHERN AND WESTERN EUROPE

To facilitate the transition from the Romance language-speaking countries of Southern and Western Europe to the Germanic countries in the northwest of the continent, the surname patterns of the following countries will be described in this section: Italy, Spain, Portugal, France, Belgium, the Netherlands, and Germany. The transition occurs in Belgium, a country divided into the French-speaking Walloon Region in the south, bordering France, and the Dutch-speaking Flanders in the north, close to the Netherlands.

ITALIAN

In ancient Rome, the use of *tria nomina* (three names) was adopted, which consisted of *praenomen, nomen,* and *cognomen* (Johnston, 1903). The *praenomen* (forename) is a personal name. The *nomen* is a hereditary surname that identifies the *gens*, or the family group the person belongs to. The *praenomen* and the *nomen* constitute the essential elements of the name. They could be followed by a *cognomen*, which was used to further identify the individual. It could be a nickname that referred to a physical characteristic or a personality trait or it could be hereditary, used to further identify the family as part of a larger genealogical branch. The *tria nomina* Quintus Tullius Rufus might belong to the fifth born (Quintus) in the Tullius family who was a redhead (Rufus). Many of the famous ancient Romans are known only by their *cognomina* (Cicero, Caesar, Trajan, Hadrian).

Women in ancient Rome were identified by the feminine form of the nomen and the genitive form of the father's cognomen, or their husband's, if married. If there was more than one daughter in the family, an ordinal numeral (Secunda or Tertia) or a comparative adjective (Maior or Minor) might be added as a cognomen (not a praenomen as for males).

The *tria nomina* Roman custom was lost in the Middle Ages, when people were known by their baptismal name, their *praenomen*. As populations grew, especially in large metropolitan areas, the need arose to distinguish among individuals with the same Christian name, so gradually they began to adopt a second name.

The evolution of the surname was not a uniform process. At first, early in the 11th century, rich Venetian families were able to buy surnames. Over the next few centuries, their use became commonplace among all families, from large cities to small villages. Surnames were a necessity for the Church when marking baptisms, marriages and burials. In 1564, the Council of Trent made it mandatory for parish priests to record all such milestones with both names.

The most noteworthy fact of Italian surnames is the sheer number of them. It is estimated that there are approximately 350,000 surnames in Italy (Donati, 2022). Not only are there many categories of names, but they are multiplied by frequent prefixes (***La, Lo, Da, De, Del, Della, Delle, Di***) and suffixes that indicate a wide variety of diminutives and gender and number variants. The abundance of diminutives in the Italian language is manifest in its surname patterns (***-ini, -ino, -etti, -etto, -ello,*** and ***-illo).*** Other suffixes that indicate specific traits of an individual— ***-one*** (big), ***-accio*** (big/bad), and ***-ucci*** (descendant of)—further contribute to the vast array of surname variations.

The evolution of Italian surnames follows the patterns of many western cultures. Most Italian surnames are derived from the first name of the head of household. Patronymic and occasionally matronymic surnames often begin with the preposition ***di*** or its variants ***de*** or ***d'*** (before vowels), that denotes possession (offspring of), i.e. DiGiovanni, DiPaola, De Luca, D'Ettore. Some such names bear a Latin genitive ending of a parent's name.

- De Andreis – offspring of Andrea
- De Bastiani – offspring of Sebastiano/Bastiano
- De Laurentiis – offspring of Lorenzo

Others use the Latin genitive ending without the preposition.

- Adami – offspring of Adamo
- Agosti – offspring of Agosto

Toponymic (also known as **geographic** or **habitational**) surnames, which indicate the geographic origin of a family, account for more than one third of Italian surnames (Abbruzzese, Genovese, Mantovani, Tarantino, Veronese). Each of these names might present variations that indicate gender and number (Romana, Romano, Romani). Others use a preposition of place (from): De Genova, Di Palermo, Da Padova. So a person whose ancestors come from Naples could bear any of these surnames: Di Napoli, De Napoli, Napoli, Napolitani, Napolitano, Napoletani, Napoletano.

Ethnic surnames point to the national origin of an ancestor.

- Albanese, Albanesi – Albania
- Bulgari – Bulgaria
- Francese, Franzese – France
- Greco – Greece
- Inglese – England
- LoSchiavo – the Slav
- Russo – Russia
- Scotti – Scotland
- Tedesco – Germany

- Turchi – Turkey
- Ungaro, Ungaretti – Hungary

Topographic surnames indicate a feature of the land where an ancestor might have dwelt.

- Costa, Di Costa – a coastal region
- Fontana – near a spring
- Marini, Marino – the sea
- Monti, DelMonte – the mountains

Occupational surnames describe the occupation of an ancestor.

- Abate – abbot, priest
- Barbieri – barber
- Buffone – jester, clown
- Cacciatore – hunter
- Carbone – coal miner
- Carpenteri – carpenter
- Coiro – leather worker
- Contadino – farmer
- Cuocco, Cuoco – cook
- Fabbri, Fabbro – blacksmith
- Ferraro, Ferrara, Ferrari, Ferrero – metal worker
- Laguardia – sentry, sentinel, guard
- Pastore – shepherd
- Sarto, Sartore – tailor
- Scarpa – shoemaker
- Speziale – grocer, spice seller
- Vaccaro – cowherd

Descriptive surnames are often derivations of nicknames. They usually refer to appearance—height, weight, complexion, hair color, personality traits, habits. Many such surnames have the prefix (definite article) ***lo*** or ***la***.

- Basso, Bassi – short
- Bianco – white, pale
- Biondi, LoBiondo – blond, fair-haired
- Bruno, Bruni – brown, brunette
- LaForte – the strong one
- Gentile – gentle, kind
- Grasso – fat

- Grosso, Grossi – large
- LoGalbo – the yellow (fair) one
- Longo – long, tall
- LoPiano – the still/slow one
- Manco, Mancuso – left-handed
- Negri, Neri, Negrini – black
- Ricci – curly
- Rossi, Rossini, Roselli – red-haired
- Sapienti – wise
- Sordi – deaf
- Vitale – lively

Animal names are included in this category as they were often given based on certain personality traits. A large number of Italian surnames are either names of animals or derivations from them.

- Agnelli, Agnellini – lamb
- Bove, Boveri – ox
- Cavallo – horse
- Colombo, Colombi – dove
- Falco – falcon
- Gallo – rooster
- Gatto, Gatti, Gattini – cat
- Leone, Leoni – lion
- Lupo, Lupino – wolf
- Mosconi, Moschella – housefly
- Orsi, Orsini – bear
- Palumbo – pigeon
- Pavone, Pavoni – peacock
- Pesce, Pesci – fish
- Serpico – serpent
- Tortora – turtledove
- Vacca, Vaccaro – cow
- Vespa – wasp

The practice of assigning surnames to **abandoned children** took various forms. One of the most common surnames given to foundlings is Esposito or one of its variants, especially prevalent in the Naples area. It is derived from the Latin verb *expōnere* (to place outside). The name *Della Casagrande* points to the *ospizio*, the hospital or hospice where the baby was abandoned. Other such surnames might be Abbandonato, Degli

Innocenti, Didio, Del Mondo, Incogniti, Infante, Orfanelli, Trovatelli, Della Donna, Della Fortuna, Dell'Amore, or the name of a month, presumably of the month the baby was abandoned (Aprile, Febbraio, Settembre, etc.). Other foundlings bore the names of objects from nature, including animals, a practice common to the northern part of the country.

- Monti – mountains
- DelMonte – from the mountains
- Pietri – stones
- Rosa – rose
- Garofano – carnation

The 10 most common surnames in Italy according to Adams (2018) are:

1. **Rossi** (red)
2. **Russo** (Russian)
3. **Ferrari** (metal worker)
4. **Esposito** (denotes a child who was rescued after being abandoned by parents)
5. **Bianchi** (white)
6. **Romano** (Roman)
7. **Colombo** (dove, possibly dove keeper)
8. **Ricci** (rich)
9. **Marino** (of the sea)
10. **Greco** (Greek)

SPANISH

As in most European countries, hereditary Spanish surnames (*apellidos*) first came into use around the 12th century, when the increase in population and mobility to larger cities made it necessary to distinguish among people with the same given name.

The most characteristic feature of Spanish names is the use of double-barreled surnames—the father's followed by the mother's in most cases. So, for instance, if Luis Enrique Rodríguez Nieto marries María Elena García Moreno, their daughter Cecilia would be named Cecilia Rodríguez García. Over the past two decades, gender equality laws in Spain have aimed to bring equity to naming patterns, specifically in allowing parents to decide the order of surnames for their children, with the requirement that all siblings in a family have the same order (Boletín Oficial del Estado, 1999). This law was further expanded in 2017 (Europa Press, 2017).

Spanish naming patterns have not always been this predictable. Sometimes boys adopted their father's surname while girls took their mother's. Prior to the 18th century, matrilineal surname transmission was not uncommon. Sometimes children were given a grandparent's surname in the hope of receiving a larger inheritance or simply because it sounded more genteel. It is believed that the Castilian double surname tradition began with noble families and did not become widespread until the 1800s.

In the 16th century, the Spanish adopted the conjunction ***y*** (*and*) to separate the two surnames (Goya y Lucientes, Bourbon y Parma, Ortega y Gasset), a practice that is rarely used today, except in Catalan names (with the conjunction ***i***). Aside from sounding aristocratic, its use served to avoid confusion in cases where one or both surnames were composite names (Mauricio López-Trujillo y del Mar) or when the first surname could be interpreted as a second first name (Pedro Martín Amaya → Pedro Martín y Amaya). Similarly, the preposition ***de*** could be used as a conjunction to differentiate between the two last names (Sancho Fernández de Tejada, Vasco Nuñez de Balboa) or placed before the first surname to avoid it being mistaken for a second first name (Pedro de Martín Amaya). When used as a preposition, *de* (of, from) could show noble lineage (de la Cerda) or geographic origin (de León).

As expected, the largest category of surnames is **patronymic**, or **matronymic** when the father is unknown or the mother's family name is more prestigious or better sounding. For the most part, Spanish patronymic surnames were formed by adding the suffixes ***-ez, -az, -is, -oz*** or ***-os*** to the father's given name.

- Díaz – offspring of Diego
- Estévez – offspring of Esteban
- González, Gonzales – offspring of Gonzalo
- Jiménez – offspring of Jimeno, Ximeno or Ximena
- Márquez – offspring of Marco or Marcos
- Muñoz – offspring of Muño (medieval name)
- Pérez – offspring of Pedro
- Rodríguez – offspring of Rodrigo
- Ruiz – offspring of Ruy/Roy (diminutive of Rodrigo)

- Vásquez, Vázquez – offspring of Vasco
- Velázquez – offspring of Velasco
- Vélez – offspring of Vela

Some patronyms are identical to the parent's first name (Martín, Vidal, Andrés, Antonio, Bautista, Duarte, Alonso, Lucas, María) or derived from it (Sanz, from Sancho; Macías, from Mateo).

Topographic surnames constitute another large category of Spanish surnames. Many are derived from words that describe the physical characteristics of a place of origin.

- Aguilar – eagles' nest
- Castillo – castle
- Cruz – cross
- Fuentes – fountain
- Iglesias – churches
- Mendoza – cold mountain in the Basque language
- Morales – blackberry groves
- Olmos, del Olmo – elm trees
- Rivera – riverbank
- Roble, Robles, Robledo – oak trees
- Serrano – highlander
- Soto, de Soto, Desoto – forest/grove of trees
- Torres, de la Torre, Delatorre – tower
- Valle, del Valle – valley
- Vega, de la Vega – meadow

Toponymic surnames may refer to a city or town of origin.

- Castilla – the province of Castille
- Dávila, De Ávila, d'Ávila, Ávila – the city of Avila
- de León – the city of León
- Lugo, de Lugo – the town of Lugo
- Navarro – the community of Navarra
- Ortega – the village of Ortega

Unlike Italian and French, Spanish toponyms rarely point to another country as the origin of a surname. Names like Franco and Marroquín are rare in Spain.

Occupational last names were initially derived from a person's job or trade, the majority of which represent common occupations, often given by nobles to the commoners who worked for them.

- Barbero – barber
- Barros – an artisan, builder, or someone who worked with clay; this could also be a topographic name for someone who lived near a muddy area.
- Cabrera, Cabrero – goat herder
- Cisneros – one who sold or kept swans
- Guerrero – warrior
- Herrera, Herrero, Ferrera – blacksmith
- Marín – sailor
- Molina, Molinero – mill owner
- Romero – pilgrim
- Torrero – bullfighter
- Vicario – vicar
- Zapatero – shoemaker

Conversely, members of the nobility chose for themselves occupational surnames that denoted their title or position.

- Caballero, Cavallero – knight, horseman
- Duque – duke
- Hidalgo – nobleman
- Marqués, Márquez – marquis; also a patronym, offspring of Marcos
- Reyes – kings, royalty

These names could also have been used to designate those who worked in the household of a nobleman, a knight or at a royal court.

The smallest category is made up of **descriptive** surnames, which are derived from an individual's physical or personality trait, that often became a nickname.

- Bravo – brave
- Calvo – bald
- Cano – gray-haired
- Cortés – courteous
- Delgado – thin
- Garza – long-legged (heron)
- Grande – large

- Hermosillo – derived from *hermoso* (beautiful)
- Leal – loyal
- Moreno – dark
- Rubio – blonde

Historically, descriptive surnames were sometimes given as a form of insult—Orejón (big ears)—so it stands to reason that most of them did not survive over time. The ones that did were either positive or neutral.

The process of assigning surnames to **abandoned** children was an especially pesky problem for civil registrars because they not only had to come up with one, but two surnames. Some were named after the town where they were found as a first surname and after a specific place within the town as their second surname—Iglesias (church), Cruz (cross). Some were given the surname Gracia or de Gracia because they were thought to have survived by the grace of God, or the surname Deulofeu (made by God, in Catalan). A common surname given to foundlings was Expósito/Expósita, from the Latin *expositus* (exposed, meaning *abandoned*), which marked them and their descendants as illegitimate, therefore of a lower social class. To right this wrong, a 1921 Spanish law made it legal for all citizens named Expósito to change their surname (El Almanaque, n.d.). Abandoned babies could also be assigned surnames after the saint corresponding to their birthday.

In the case of illegitimate children, when the father is either unknown or refuses to accept paternity, the child is given both of the mother's surnames in either order or a combination of the surnames of the grandparents.

BASQUE surnames originate in the Basque Country (*Euskal* in Basque, *País Vasco* in Spanish) and Navarre, located in the western Pyrenees, straddling the border between France and Spain. The Northern Basque Country is part of France and the Southern Basque Country is part of Spain. The (Southern) Basque Country, as the rest of Spain, follows the two-surname pattern—the paternal, followed by the maternal, although the maternal-first order is becoming more common.

Given that the top 10 most frequent surnames in Spain constitute more than 18% of those of the total population (Lang, 2014), it is not surprising that most of them are also in the top 10 in the Basque Country, which would make patronymics the most common category of surnames there. However, if we examine only Basque surnames, we find that the majority are topographic, referring to some aspect of the family home (*etxea*).

Patronymic surnames constitute a minor category. The patronymic suffix ***-iz***, derived from the Latin genitive ending *-is*, is attached to a male ancestor's first name: Ortiz (from Orti), Enecoiz (from Eneko), Miqueleiz (from Mikele), Sanoiz (from Sanso).

A **topographic** surname can denote a characteristic of the family homestead or of the topography of the place where the house was built. Many of these surnames are compound names made up of two elements—either two nouns, an adjective and a noun, or a number and a noun.

- Arriortua – stone orchard, from *harri* (stone) + *ortua* (orchard)
- Bolívar – valley mill, from *bolu* (mill) + *ibar* (valley)
- Bostirieta – five cities, from *bost* (five) + *iri* (city)
- Etxebarria (Echevarría in Spanish) – the new house, from *etxe* (house) + *barri* (new) + *-a* (the)
- Garaikoetxea – the house in the heights, from *garai* (height) + *etxe* (house) + *-a* (the)
- Larraburu – pasture at the summit, from *larra/larre* (pasture) + *buru* (summit)
- Loyola – muddy smithery, from *loi* (mud) + *ola* (smithery)
- Madariaga – place planted with pears, from *madari* (pears) + -*aga* (place of)
- Mendikoetxea – the house in the mountains, from *mendi* (mountain) + *etxe* (house) + *-a* (the)
- Mendoza – cold mountain, from *mendi* (mountain) + *hotza* (cold)
- Salazar – old hall, from *sala* (hall) + *zahar/zar* (old)
- Saratxaga – willow place, from *saratze* (willow) + *-aga* (place of)
- Unamuno – cowherd on the hill, from *unai* (cowherd) + *muno* (hill)
- Zubizarreta – old bridge, from *zubia* (bridge) + *zahar* (old)

Other simpler geographical Basque surnames are:

- Amaya – probably from *amai* (end) + *-a* (the)
- Ayala – from *ai* (slope, hillside) + *ala* (pasture); also, the Spanish equivalent of the Basque town *Aiara*
- Goya – from *goi* (top)

- Guevara – toponymic surname from Gebala, in the Basque province of Araba
- Ibarra – meadow, valley
- Orozco – toponym based on the Basque mountain called Oroz

More than two elements can be combined to form surnames: Urberoaga – hot water place, from *ur* (water) + *bero* (hot) + *-aga* (place of). Sometimes two surnames were combined into one, yielding extremely long ones: Elorduizapaterietxe – Elordui + Zapaterietxe. The longest surname recorded in Spain is Burionagonatotoricagageazcoechea, formed by Buriona + Gonatar + Totorika + Beazcoetxea (Albaigès, 1995).

In some Basque provinces it was uncommon for a surname to be the same as a town of residence, unless it belonged to a foundling. A common such name might be Bilbao. In other Basque provinces, such as Alava and Navarra, a town could be used along with a last name if preceded by the particle ***de***, indicating a toponym (Juan García de Aiara/Ayala).

To better illustrate Basque names, here are some examples of actual Basque people (Buber, 2020):

- Joseph Etcheverry Oxoteguy
- Josu Aguirre Gabiria
- Pedro Oiarzabal
- Pedro Uberuaga Zabala
- Blas Antonio Telleria Goya
- Carmen Larrabeiti Urquiza
- Nestor Basterretxea Arzadun

CATALAN surnames are diffused throughout the Catalan-speaking areas in Catalonia, Valencia, the Balearic Islands, Andorra. These territories abide by Spanish naming customs. Compared to Spanish surnames, where the top 10 most frequent surnames are held by 18.1% of the total population, Catalan surnames are much more diverse; the 10 most frequent surnames make up only 8% of all Catalan surnames (Solé-Morata et al, 2015).

Catalan surname patterns are similar to those in the rest of Spain. However, the actual names are distinctive in that they contain or end in sounds not normally found in Castilian Spanish (Wagadugu, 2006).

-uig, -oig, -ig (pronounced /-utch/, /-otch/, /-itch/), as in Puig and Roig

-sch (pronounced /-sk/), as in Bosch

-ch (pronounced /k/), as in Domenech and Subirachs

ll (pronounced /ly/), as in Guillem and Llobet

x (pronounced /sh/), as in Rexach

The conjunction ***i*** (and), the equivalent of the Spanish *y*, is commonly used to join the two surnames. To better illustrate Catalan names, here are the names of five famous painters:

- Josep Tapiró i Baró (1836-1913)
- Marià Fortuny i Marsal (1838-1874) – full name: Marià Josep Maria Bernat Fortuny i Marsal, known more simply as Marià Fortuny or Mariano Fortuny
- Eliseu Meifrèn (1857-1940) – full name: Eliseu Meifrèn i Roig
- Joan Miró (1893-1983) – full name: Joan Miró i Ferrà
- Salvador Dalí (1904-1989) – full name: Salvador Domingo Felipe Jacinto Dalí i Domènech, primer marqués de Púbol

According to the National Institute of Statistics of Spain (Europa Press, 2021), eight out of the 10 most common surnames end in ***-ez***. These 10 names constitute 18.1% of the total population. In view of these statistics, the use of double surnames is not simply a way to honor the ancestors of both parents, but a practical way to differentiate among several people with the same first surname. This is in fact the main reason for the rise of surnames in the first place.

The 10 most frequent surnames in Spain in 2020 were (Europa Press, 2021):

1. **García** (possibly from the Basque hartz=bear, or see below for alternate interpretations)
2. **González** (offspring of Gonzalo)
3. **López** (offspring of Lope, from Latin Lupus=wolf)
4. **Sánchez** (offspring of Sancho, from Latin sanctus=holy)
5. **Gómez** (offspring of Gome)
6. **Jimenez** (offspring of Jimeno, Ximeno or Ximena)
7. **Ruiz** (offspring of Ruy/Roy, diminutives of Rodrigo)
8. **Moreno** (dark)

9. **Álvarez** (offspring of Álvaro)
10. **Gutierrez** (offspring of Gutierre)

The most frequent surname in Spain, García, happens to be one of uncertain origin. Some believe it to be patronymic, derived from a medieval personal name. It appears in medieval records in the Latin form of *Garsea*, possibly of pre-Roman origin. Another supposition is that it derives from the Basque adjective *garze(a)* (young) or the Basque noun *(h)artz* (bear), or a combination of the two—*gartze (h)artz* (young bear) (Powell, 2019).

Portuguese

Before Roman times, the natives of present-day Portugal used a single name, then a single name and a patronym. Toward the end of the first century CE, the practice of the *tria nomina* (*praenomen, nomen, cognomen*) began to gradually be used. See explanation under Italian Surnames.

It is not unusual for Portuguese names to be quite long. According to law, people can have a maximum of six names—one or two first names and up to four family names; each name can be simple or composite. However, unofficially, someone might have two given names and anywhere from two to ten, or even more surnames. The choice and order of surnames do not follow a standard method, although most commonly the first names are followed by the mother's last name(s) and then the father's. This is the opposite of the surname order in Spanish-speaking countries, where the father's last name precedes the mother's.

Historically, girls were given their mother's surnames and boys received their father's. It was also common to give children both of their parents' surnames, first the mother's then the father's, which they retained for life.

In the 1970s, Portuguese and Brazilian women were given the option of whether or not to take their spouse's name after marriage. This right was given to men in Portugal at the same time and in Brazil in 2002. Most people, however, choose to keep their birth names their entire lives. As of 2014, only 41% of women and 4% of men in Portugal opt for their spouse's surname (Catarina, 2018). In Brazil, if a woman chooses to adopt her husband's surname(s), she may keep or exclude her own surnames. In

Portugal, people are not allowed to drop their birth names, so if they choose to take their spouse's surname, they must attach it to their own, thus ending up with a very long name. So if a woman named Maria de Lurdes Santos Almeida marries a man named José António Silva Henriques and they both want to take each other's surnames, their names might be Maria de Lurdes Santos Almeida Henriques and José António Silva Henriques Almeida, or some variation of this. Imagine the situation where these people used all four surnames (for each of their grandparents) and decided to adopt their spouse's surnames as well. If they had children, they could decide on a simple or compound first name and at least two surnames. The simplest might be Rita Almeida Henriques, but there is no limit to the possibilities, both in length and order.

Most surnames are either patronymic, geographical or religious. Others are descriptive or occupational.

Patronymic surnames are derived from the father's given name by adding a suffix, most commonly ***-es*** (son of), but also ***-ez*** or simply ***-s***.

- Álvares, Alves – son of Álvaro
- Esteves – son of Estevão (Steven)
- Fernandes – son of Fernão/Fernando
- Gonçalves – son of Gonçalo
- Henriques – son of Henrique (Henry)
- Lopes – son of Lopo
- Marques – son of Marco/Marcos
- Martins – son of Martinho (Martin)
- Mendes – son of Mendo
- Nunes – son of Nuno
- Rodrigues – son of Rodrigo
- Simões –son of Simão (Simon)

Some patronyms are identical to given names; these are more common in Brazil than Portugal (Alonso, Fernando, Luis/Luiz, Lourenco, João). Some, such as Duarte, Garcia, Godinho, were originally given names, but they are used today in Brazil almost exclusively as surnames.

Geographical surnames, also referred to as locational, habitational, topographic, or toponymic, constitute a large percentage of Portuguese surnames. Habitational or toponymic surnames are derived from the name of the place where an ancestor lived, while topographic names often refer to topographic features of that place of origin. Often a place may have been named after a topographic feature, thus a surname could be considered either topographic or toponymic/habitational, or both. Some common surnames in this category are:

- Almeida – from the town of Almeida
- Campos – meadows, fields
- Carvalho – oak tree
- Costa – the coast
- Da Rocha – from near the rock
- De Oliveira – from near the olive tree
- Gouveia – from the city of Gouveia
- Macedo – from *macedo* (apple grove, from *maça*=apple)
- Medeiros – from any of the villages by that name (*medeiro*=haystack, referring to an area for stacking maze)
- Mendonça – from the city of Mendonça (Basque origin)
- Nogueira – from near walnut trees (*nogueira*=walnut tree, from Latin *nucarius, nux*=nut)
- Pedreira – quarry
- Pereira – pear tree
- Pinheiro – pine tree
- Ribeiro – river
- Silva, Da Silva – from any of several places named Silva, from the Latin *silva* (thicket, wood), or someone who lived near or in a forest
- Sousa, Souza – from near the River Sousa (salty place)
- Teixeira – from any of several places in Portugal and Galicia, Spain (spelled Teijeira), derived from *teixo* (yew tree in Portuguese and Galician, from the Latin *taxus*).
- Vale – valley (from Latin *vallis*)

Many geographical surnames use the preposition ***de*** (from, of) by itself or in any of its contracted forms with the definite articles *o, a, os, as* (the, in its masculine singular, feminine singular, masculine plural and feminine plural forms, respectively), yielding ***do, da, dos, das*** (of the). The convention is that they be written in lower case, although occasionally they can be seen capitalized.

Religious surnames were often assumed by converts to Christianity to profess devotion to the new faith. Orphans with unknown parents or foundlings abandoned in churches and raised in Catholic orphanages were also given surnames with religious meanings. Many of them were names of saints. Others include:

- da Conceição – of the Immaculate Conception of the Virgin Mary
- da Luz/Luz – of the light, short for *Nuestra Señora da Luz* (Our Lady of the Light)
- de Deus – of God
- de Jesus – of Jesus
- do Espírito Santo – of the Holy Spirit
- dos Anjos – of the angels
- Graça – from Our Lady of Grace
- Nascimento – birth, nativity
- Santos – saints

Descriptive surnames are often derivations of nicknames, referring to a characteristic of an ancestor.

- Belo – beautiful
- Crespo – curly
- Delgado – thin (from Latin *delicatus*=delicate, tender)
- Galhardo – gallant, chivalrous
- Guerreiro – warrior, nickname for a belligerent person or a brave soldier, also an occupational name
- Lacerda – may have been a nickname for someone with long, thick hair or with ample body hair, from Portuguese and Spanish *la cerda* (bristle, horse hair)
- Magro – thin
- Pinto – of dark complexion
- Raposa/Raposo – nickname for a cunning person or someone with reddish hair, from *raposa* (fox). It could also be a habitational name from the Portuguese town of Raposa.
- Veloso – wooly or hairy

A smaller number of surnames originated from **occupations.** A metonymic occupational name is a name given after an object related to someone's occupation that the person may be identified with. For instance, Madeira is a metonymic occupational name for a carpenter, from *madeira* (wood, timber). It may also be a geographical surname, indicating origin in the island of Madeira, named after the timber that grew there. Other examples of occupational surnames are:

- Barreto – hat maker
- Cabral – goat herd
- Carneiro – shepherd
- Carreira – carter
- Farina/Farinha – miller, flour merchant
- Ferreira – blacksmith
- Leitao – keeper of pigs, or nickname (piglet)
- Machado – maker or user of hatchets (from Latin *marculus*=little hammer)
- Monteiro – hunter
- Peixeiro – fisherman, fishmonger
- Plateiro – silversmith
- Sardinha – sardine seller
- Soares – from soeiro (swineherd)

A relatively small number of surnames are derived from **animals.**

- Coelho – rabbit
- Cordeiro – young lamb
- Gama – deer/doe
- Lopes – wolf
- Raposa – fox

The 10 most common Portuguese surnames are (Forebears, 2012-2022a; Forebears, 2012-2022b):

In Portugal	**In Brazil**
1. Silva	1. da Silva
2. Santos	2. dos Santos
3. Ferreira	3. Perreira
4. Pereira	4. Alves
5. Costa	5. Ferreira
6. Oliveira	6. Rodrigues
7. Martins	7. Silva
8. Rodrigues	8. de Oliveira
9. Sousa	9. de Souza
10. Fernandes	10. Gomes

FRENCH

As in most countries in Europe, surnames were not used in France until the need for them arose, in other words, when mobility away from birth villages to cities required people to distinguish themselves from others who bore the same given name. The first surnames were recorded early in the 11th century, although they remained uncommon for several hundred years. At first, people were free to adopt any name they pleased, but in 1474, King Louis XI decreed that all family names would have to be approved by him. After that time, all names and name changes were recorded (Family Education, 2022).

Like most surnames, French surnames fall into four basic categories: patronymic, occupational, descriptive, and geographical.

Patronymic surnames constitute the most common category of surnames. In fact, with about one million patronymics, France holds the record for the country with the largest number of surnames in the world (Guinness World Records, 2020), estimated at between 800,000 and 1,200,000. Most patronymic (or matronymic) surnames come directly from the father's first name (or the mother's if the father is unknown or the mother is thought to be wealthier or more influential than the father)—Marie Girard (daughter of Girard), Henri Bernard (son of Bernard). Another way of forming a patronymic surname was to attach a prefix (***de, des, du*** or the Norman *Fitz*) or a suffix (***-eau, -elot, -elin, -elle, -elet***) to the parent's given name. These surnames were not hereditary, but changed from generation to generation. In 1539, King François I enacted an ordinance requiring all parishes to register all baptisms with an unchangeable family name. From that point on, surnames became not only mandatory, but hereditary (Alister, 2014).

Occupational surnames are the second most common type of surname. Based on the occupation or trade of a person, some of the more common ones are:

- Arsenault – gun maker/gun merchant
- Barbier – barber
- Berger – shepherd
- Bisset – weaver
- Boucher – butcher
- Boulanger – baker
- Caron – cartwright

- Charbonnier – charcoal seller
- Chatelain – constable, prison warden
- Chevalier – knight, horseman
- Chevrolet – goat keeper
- Dufour, Fournier – oven worker, baker
- Fabron – blacksmith
- Forestier – keeper of the king's forrest
- Gagne, Gagnon – farmer
- Garnier – keeper of the granary
- Lambert – lamb herder
- Leclerc – clerk, secretary
- Lefebre – craftsman
- Lefèvre – ironworker, smith
- Lemaire – the mayor
- Lemaitre – master craftsman
- Le Sueur – cobbler
- Marchant – merchant
- Martel – blacksmith, from *martel*=hammer
- Moulin, Mullins – miller
- Page – servant
- Pelletier – furrier
- Porcher – swineherd
- Sartre – tailor
- Vachon – cowherd

Descriptive surnames, based on a characteristic of an individual, can refer to distinguishing physical features or personality traits and may have been derived from nicknames.

- Alarie – all-powerful
- Allard – noble
- Anouilh – slow
- Archambeau – daring
- Bassett – low, of humble origins
- Bellamy – beautiful friend
- Blanchet – blond, pure
- Brun – with dark hair or complexion
- Camus – pug-nosed; possibly also a metonymic occupational surname for *shirt maker*
- Chauvin – bald

- Durand – enduring
- Fortin – strong
- LeBlanc – blonde, light-skinned
- Legrand – big
- Lenoir – black, dark
- Leroux – redheaded
- Moreau – dark-skinned
- Petit – small
- Proulx – brave, valiant
- Thibaut – brave, bold

Geographical surnames were a later arrival to French surname patterns, as mobility away from birth villages became more common. These newer surnames served to identify the origin of a person and sometimes replaced the original surname and were passed on to the next generations. This name often described the **topographical** feature of a place of origin.

- Beaulieu – a beautiful place
- Beaumont – beautiful mountain
- Beausoleil – beautiful sun, a sunny place
- Chastain – chestnut tree
- De la Rue – from the street
- Delacroix – from/of the cross
- Deschamps – from the fields
- Desjardins – from the gardens
- Desmarais – from the marsh
- Dubois – from the forest
- Dumas – from the farm
- Dumont – from the mountain
- Dupont – from the bridge
- Dupuis – from the well
- Duval – from the valley
- Fontaine – fountain
- Lafitte – near the border
- Lavigne – the vineyard
- Poirier, Poirot – a pear tree or orchard

A **toponymic** surname can also originate from the name of a city in France or a country of origin (ethnic surname).

- Lallemant, Lallemand, L'allemand – German
- Langlais, Langlois – Englishman
- Litalien – Italian
- Marseille – from the city of Marseille
- Parisien – from Paris

The practice of assigning surnames to **abandoned children** was not uniform throughout history (Forez, n.d.). In the centuries before the French Revolution (1789), these surnames reflected:

- the place where the infants were found, i.e. a church (Saint Jean le Rond → le Rond), a village or a commune (Saint-Laurent-de-Chamousset → Laurent)
- a religious reference, i.e. a cross (de la Croix/Delacroix), a saint's name, based on the day of birth (Saint Martin, Saint André)
- the birth month (Janvier, Février)
- a good omen (Amour, Felicité, Bienvenu, Benoit, Bonaventure)
- the weather condition (Beaujour, Bontemps, Dusoleil, Froid, Beautemps)

At the time of the French Revolution, there was a movement, reflected in surname assignations, away from any religious reference and toward an appreciation for:

- ancient Greek culture, theater and literature (Oedipe, Hercule, Annibal, Achile, Ephése, Bérénice, Othello, Olimpe)
- astronomy (Mercure, Venus, Saturne)
- nature (Violette, Tulipe, Rossignol, Printemps, Dété)

Some forty years later, during the Restoration, there was a movement back to religious references. There were also invented surnames with no apparent specific reference (Abuer, Acaste, Abbon, Abbalouzine, Benoîte). Abandoned children were sometimes given two first names, the second of which would be used as a surname (Jean François, Pierre Pascal).

The surname Donadieu/Donnadieu (given to God) was given not only to children who were orphaned or abandoned, but also to those who were pledged to the priesthood or the convent.

Finally, in 1841, the Ministry of the Interior decreed that, to avoid discrimination, abandoned children should not be given identifiable last names, but rather common names indicative of their birth places (Dupin, Dufour, Montet, Dumas, Grange, Rousset).

The 10 most common French surnames for people born between 1891 and 1990 were (Geopatronyme, n.d.a):

1. Martin (patronymic, after the most popular French saint, Saint Martin of Tours)
2. Bernard (patronymic, from the given name, which is of Germanic origin)
3. Thomas (patronymic, from the medieval given name of Biblical origin, meaning *twin*)
4. Petit (a descriptive name, *small*)
5. Robert (patronymic, from the Germanic given name meaning *bright*)
6. Richard (patronymic, from the Germanic given name meaning *powerful, strong*)
7. Durand (a descriptive name, *steadfast*, from the Old French *durant* and Latin *durandus*=enduring)
8. Dubois (a geographic name for someone living in a forest, from *du*=from + *bois*=wood)
9. Moreau (a descriptive type of name meaning *dark-skinned*; literally, *son of the Moor*)
10. Laurent (a geographic name; from the Roman surname *Laurentius*, which meant from *Laurentum*, an ancient Roman city)

There was little change over the next 75 years in the most common French surnames. The one noteworthy fact among the top 10 surnames for those born between 1966 and 1990 (Geopatronyme, n.d.b) is the presence of the name García, the most common surname in Spain.

1. **Martin** – from personal name
2. **Bernard** – from personal name
3. **Thomas** – from personal name
4. **Robert** – from personal name
5. **Petit** – small
6. **Dubois** – from the forest
7. **Richard** – from personal name
8. **García** – the most common name in Spain
9. **Durand** – enduring

10. **Moreau** – derived from a diminutive of Maurus (dark-skinned)

The Council of Europe, an international organization committed to upholding human rights, requires its member nations to adopt equality of rights in the transmission of family names. Since 2005, partners are free to choose their names after marriage. Likewise, a child may be given either parent's surname or both, provided that it's used consistently (Légifrance, 2021).

Belgian

The country of Belgium is divided into three autonomous regions: the Dutch-speaking Flemish Region (Flanders) in the north, the French-speaking Walloon Region (Wallonia) in the south, and the Brussels-Capital Region, an officially bilingual enclave located within the monolingual Flanders.

The Dutch-speaking Flemish people of the north, who constitute about 60% of the population, bear surnames that are quite similar to the Dutch in the Netherlands, whereas the French-speaking Walloons in the south of Belgium, who make up less than 40% of the total population, tend to have French surnames.

Some of the most common surnames in Belgium are **patronymic**. The Dutch/Flemish surnames follow the Netherlanders' traditions of adding a suffix (***-s, -sens, -ssens*** or ***-x***) to the given name of an ancestor, whereas the Walloons follow the French custom of using the given name as such without an added ending. Here are some examples of patronymic surnames in Belgium.

Dutch/Flemish

- Christiaans, Christiaens – descendent of Cristiaen (Christian)
- Goossens – descendent of Goossen
- Hendrikx – descendent of Hendrik (Henry)
- Janssens – descendent of Jan (John)
- Martens, Mertens – descendent of Marten, Merten (Martin)
- Merckx – descendent of Merck (Mark)
- Peeters – descendent of Peeter (Peter)
- Willems – descendent of Willem (William)

French

- Antoine
- Bertrand
- Gérard
- Laurent
- Martin
- Mathieu
- Pierre
- Robert

Like Dutch surnames in the Netherlands and in several other countries, Belgian surnames use *tussenvoegsels*—particles consisting of the preposition *from/of* with or without a definite article or just the definite article—between a given name and a surname (Hoitink, 2013). In Flemish/Dutch they are usually represented by ***van, van der*** (often reduced to ***ver***), ***van de*** or ***van den***, and in French by ***de*** or ***du***. The difference between the *tussenvoegsels* in the Netherlands and in Belgium is that in the Netherlands they are not capitalized when preceded by a name or an initial and they are not part of the indexing process, whereas in Belgium they are. So, if you wanted to look up Geert van der Aart's phone number in the Netherlands, you would look under the letter A, but if he was a Flemish man living in Belgium, you would find him under letter V, and his surname might be Van der Aart, Ver Aart, Veraart, Vanaart, or something similar. This concatenation of two or more parts into a single name distinguishes Flemish Dutch names from their Netherlander counterparts.

In the case of French surnames, in Belgium as in France, the *tussenvoegsel* containing the preposition ***de*** and a definite article (***du, de la, des***) is integrated into the name itself, as in: Delacroix, Dubois, Dupont, Desjardins. The same happens with the definite article in any of its forms (***le, l', la***): Lacroix, Langlais, Legrand.

It is important to point out that while the particle ***de*** is the preposition *from/of* in French, in Dutch it is the definite article *the*. So when we see the name De Boer, we should be able to recognize that it is a Dutch name beginning with a definite article, therefore Boer must be a noun, most probably an occupation. Indeed, it means *the farmer*.

Here are some names derived from **topographical features**, most of which contain *tussenvoegsels*.

Dutch/Flemish

- Eikenboom – oak tree
- Peerenboom – pear tree
- Rietveld – red field
- Roggeveen – rye peat
- Van Beek – from the brook
- Van Dalen – from the valley
- Vandroogenbroeck – from the dry marshes (Brussels was built on dry marshes)
- Van Rompa / Van Rompaey / Van Rompay / Van Rompaye / Van Rompu / Van Rompuy – from the wide path (*ruum*=wide, spacious + *pat*=path, in Middle Dutch)
- Vermeulen – from the mill
- Vervloet – from the stream

French

- Beaulieu – beautiful place
- Chastain – chestnut tree
- Deforest – from the forest
- Deschamps – from the fields
- Desrosiers – from the rose bushes
- Dubois – from the woods (forest)
- Dumas – from the farm
- Dumont – from the mountain
- Dupuis – from the well
- Duval – from the valley
- Lavigne – the vineyard

Many family names are derived from the occupation of an ancestor. Table 1 lists some common occupational surnames and their equivalents in the two main languages of Belgium.

Table 1. Common occupational surnames in Belgium

Flemish/Dutch	French	English translation
De Bakker	Boulanger, Fournier	baker
Beenhouwer	Boucher	butcher
De Boer	Gagne, Gagnon	farmer
Brouwer, Blonder	Brasseur	brewer
Jaager, Jaeger	Chasseur	hunter
(De) Klerk	Leclercq	clerk
Koopman	Marchant	merchant
Molenaar, Molnar	Monnier, Du Moulin	miller
Schoenmaker	Lesueur, Savatier	cobbler
Slootmaekers	Serrurier	locksmith
Smet, Smid	Lefèvre, Fabron	smith, blacksmith
Snijder	Sartre, Sartain	tailor
Spijker	Clavel, Cloutier	nail maker/seller
Timmermans	Charpentier	carpenter
Visser	Barbeau (type of fish)	fisherman
Weidman	Berger, Bergeron	shepherd

There are, of course, many other occupational surnames that are specific to each group.

Dutch/Flemish

- Bleecker, Bleeker – bleacher, launderer
- De Kok – the cook
- Haak – peddler
- Hoedemaeker, Hoedemaekers, Hoedemaker, Hoedemakers – hat maker
- Hosekin, Hoskins – maker or seller of hose
- Houtkooper – wood buyer
- Huitema – wood cutter
- Knickerbacker – baker of clay marbles
- Metsalaer – mason
- Rademaker, Rademakers, Ramaker, Rameckers – wheel maker
- Schrijnemaekers, Schrijnemakers – cabinet maker
- Slootmaekers, Slootmakers – locksmith

French

- Barbier – barber
- Bisset – weaver
- Bouvier – herdsman
- Capon – poultry farmer
- Caron – cartwright
- Charbonier – charcoal seller
- Chevalier – knight, horseman
- Chevrolet – goat keeper
- Lambert – lamb herder
- Lemaitre – master craftsman
- Pelletier – furrier
- Vachon – cowherd

A smaller group of surnames are **descriptive**, derived from a word or words evoking a person's physical characteristic or personality trait.

Flemish/Dutch

- Baert – beard (may refer to a bearded person or a barber)
- Degroote, DeGroote – the big one
- Devos – the fox, attributed to a sly, devious person (concatenation of De Vos)

- De Witte – the white (may refer to a blond or white-haired person)
- Hecht – nickname for a rapacious, greedy person
- Klein – small, little
- Vroom – pious, devout

French

- Archambault – bold, genuine
- Ballamy – beautiful friend
- Blanc – white (may refer to someone with white or blond hair)
- Chauvin – bald
- Durand – enduring (nickname for a stubborn person)
- Gros – thick, big, fat
- Petit – small, little
- Proulx – brave, valiant

Table 2 shows the 10 most frequent surnames in the entire country as well as in the Flemish and Wallonian regions and in the cosmopolitan, multicultural Brussels-Capital Region (Statbel, n.d.).

Table 2. The 10 most frequent surnames in Belgium by region

All Belgium	Flanders (north)	Wallonia (south)	Brussels-Capital Region
1. Peeters	1. Peeters	1. Dubois	1. Diallo
2. Janssens	2. Janssens	2. Lambert	2. Bah
3. Maes	3. Maes	3. Martin	3. Barry
4. Jacobs	4. Jacobs	4. Dupont	4. Sow
5. Mertens	5. Willems	5. Simon	5. Nguyen
6. Willems	6. Mertens	6. Leclercq	6. Janssens
7. Claes	7. Claes	7. Dumont	7. Dubois
8. Goossens	8. Wouters	8. Laurent	8. Peeters
9. Wouters	9. Goossens	9. Lejeune	9. Martin
10. De Smet	10. De Smet	10. Renard	10. Benali

It is interesting to note the striking similarity between the top 10 surnames in Flanders and in the whole of Belgium. None of the top 10 surnames of Wallonia made the list, although the top two, Dubois and Lambert, figure in the next group of 10, at 13 and 17, respectively. The Brussels-Capital Region, which, since its inception in 1989, has become increasingly ethnically diverse, counts among its top 10 surnames only two Dutch and two French surnames; the majority of the rest are north and west African.

Dutch

Prior to the 19th century, family names were not required in the Netherlands. To distinguish among several people with the same given name, patronymics were used by adding 'son of' or 'daughter of' to an individual's father's given name. These surnames were not hereditary. Dutch people who migrated to New Amsterdam (present day New York) used patronymics until 1687, when the British mandated the use of hereditary family names. In the Netherlands, permanent surnames were adopted gradually starting around the 15th century, but they did not become commonplace until Napoleon annexed the country in 1811 and mandated their use (Schulze, 2008).

In the olden days, Dutch tradition required married women to hyphenate their husband's surname with their own (his then hers) in social situations, although legally, they maintained their birth names all their lives. In modern times, married partners can choose either one of their surnames or a hyphenated one. However, in practice, women choose to either keep their surname or hyphenate the two, the husband's followed by the wife's, while men tend to keep their full birth names. Married parents decide the children's surnames, which must be the same for all the children in the family.

Dutch surnames may be derived from a father's or ancestor's, occupations, geographical locations, or personal characteristics. Some people chose to make their **patronymic** names permanent and hereditary for all successive generations by adding a suffix to the progenitor's given name or nickname. These suffixes varied across the 12 different Dutch provinces, but included ***-s, -se, -sen, -szen*** or ***-x***. Of these, the suffixes ***-s*** and ***-sen*** were common in all the provinces. Here are some examples:

- Aalders – son of Aldert
- Adrianszen – son of Adriaan
- Albers, Alberts, Albertszen – son of Albert
- Andriessen – son of Andries
- Antoniszen, Teuniszen – son of Antonisz, son of Teunizs (diminutive of Antony)
- Dennysen, Nyssen – son of Denys, son of Nys (diminutive of Denys)
- Dircks, Dircksens, Dirkse, Dirksen, Dirkx – son of Dirk
- Jans, Jansen, Janson, Janssen, Janssens, Janzen – son of Jan
- Jansens, Jansing, Jansingh, Jansink – son of Jansen
- Lucassen – son of Lucas
- Matthysse, Matthyssen, Thyssen – son of Matthys, son of Thys (diminutive of Matthys)
- Paulissen – son of Paulis (Paul)
- Pietersen – son of Pieter
- Romeijnsen – son of Romein/Romeijn/Romijn
- Willemsen – son of Willem (William)

Others chose a clan name as a permanent surname. They were formed by adding a suffix (*-ena, -enga, -ing, -inga, -ink, -ma*) to the name of the original owner. Table 3 shows the distribution of clan names in the various provinces (Hoitink, 2005).

Table 3. Clan name distribution in Dutch provinces

Suffix	Clan names	Provinces
-ena	Bultena, Matena, Wartena	Friesland Groningen
-enga	Biewenga, Kruizenga, Sikkenga	Drenthe Groningen
-ing	Abbing, Mekking, Schuiling	Drenthe Groningen
-inga	Huizinga, Abbinga, Fokkinga	Friesland Groningen
-ink	Hoitink, Meerdink, Hesselink	Overijssel Gelderland
-ma	Reitsma, Hoeksema, Miedema	Friesland

In some provinces, clan names were transferred to the farms. Those who bore a given clan name were not necessarily descendants of the original owners, but may have descended from people who lived or worked on the farm. Some farm names can be recognized from the prepositions ***te, ter*** or ***ten*** (at) or from the suffixes ***-borg, -hof, -huis, -kamp***. Some examples of surnames derived from farm names are: Te Kolste, Terwillege, Beverborg, Lunenborg, Achtenhof, Borninkhof, Maathuis, Kamphuis, Telgenkamp, Hietkamp.

Many Dutch people took the names of their **occupations** as surnames:

- Arbeider – worker
- Baas – boss, overseer
- Bakker – baker
- Beenhouwer, Vleeschhouwer – butcher
- Bleecker – linen bleacher
- Bouwmeester – builder, architect
- Brouwer – brewer
- De Boer – the farmer
- De Klerk, Klerk, Klerken, Klerks, Klerkse, Klerkx, Klerx – clerk
- Haak – peddler
- Hacker – one who chops or cleaves
- Heeren – lord, master
- Hoedemaeker, Hoedemaekers, Hoedemaker, Hoedemakers – hat maker (*hoed*=hat)
- Houtkooper – buyer of wood
- Jaager, Jaeger – hunter
- Knickerbacker – cracker baker
- Koopman – merchant
- Kuijpers, Kuiper, Kuipers, Cuyper – cooper, barrel maker
- Meijer, Meyer – an agent for the landlord of feudal estates
- Mesman – knife maker
- Metsalaer – mason
- Mulder – miller
- Rademaker, Rademakers, Ramaker, Rameckers – wheel maker (*rad*=wheel)
- Schenck – cup bearer, wine server
- Schrijnemakers – cabinet maker (*schrijn*=box, container)
- Slootmaekers – locksmith (*slot*=lock)

- Smit, Smits, Smet, Smets, Smeets, De Smet – blacksmith, metal worker
- Snijder – tailor
- Spijker – nailsmith (*spijker*=nail)
- Timmermans – carpenter
- Visser – fisherman
- Weidman – herdsman

A very large number of Dutch surnames start with one or two particles called *tussenvoegsels*, meaning insertions (between given name and surname), consisting of prepositions and/or articles, somewhat similar to the German von, the French *de*, and the Scottish *Mac* (Hoitink, 2013a). The following is a list of *tussenvoegsels*, their relative percentages of occurrence among all names that begin with these particles, and their meanings (Center for Family History, n.d.):

- ***van*** (45%) = from, of
- ***de*** (21.5%) / *den* (1.6%) = the
- ***van der*** (16.6%) / ***van den*** (7.2%) / ***van de*** (4.3%) / ***van't*** (0.5%) = from the (different inflections)
- ***ten*** (1.1%) / ***ter*** (0.8%) = at the
- ***te*** (0.4%) = at

These particles are not capitalized in the Netherlands when they are preceded by a name or an initial, but they are almost always capitalized in Belgium and other countries. So someone might say the equivalent of "My name is Pia de Groot." or "My surname is De Groot." *Tussenvoegsels* are not part of the indexing process, as they are in other countries, so these names are alphabetized according to the first capitalized letter in the surname (Groot in Pia de Groot's case).

The largest number of surnames containing *tussenvoegsels* are derived from **geographical** locations.

- De Vries – from Friesland (the Frisian)
- Van Antwerp/Van Antwerpen – from the Belgian city of Antwerp
- Van Baarle – from Baarle, a town in both the Netherlands and Belgium
- Van Bueren/Van Buren – from Buren, a small town on an island in the north of the Netherlands or a small city in the Dutch

province of Gelderland (from *bur*=house, dwelling, in Old Dutch)

- Van Daal/Van Daalen/Van Dael/Van Daele/Van Dale/Van Dalen/Vandale – from the valley (*dal*)
- Van den Akker – from the field (*akker*)
- Van den Berg/Van der Berg – from the mountain (*berg*)
- Van der Aart – from the earth (*aarde*)
- Van der Veen/Van der Ven/Van der Venne/Van Veen/Van Veenen – from the swamp/peat (*veen*)
- Van der Zee – from the sea (*zee*)
- Van de Vliert – from the elderberry (*vliert*)
- Van Dijk/Van Dyk/Dijkstra – from the dyke (*dijk*)
- Van Donk – from the hill (*donk*)
- Van Hout/Van Houte/Van Houtem/Van Houten/Van Houttum/Van Houtum/Van't Hout – from the forests (*hout*)
- Van Middelburg – from the city of Middelburg in Zeeland, the Netherlands (middle fortress)
- Van Ophoven – from any of various towns of that name in the Netherlands (upper gardens, upper courtyards)
- Van Tonder – from Tønder, a town in Denmark near the German border
- Van Willigen – from the willows (*wilga*)
- Van Winkle – from a corner (*winkel*)

There are also names derived from **geographical** locations that do not contain *tussenvoegsels.*

- Akkersdijk – the town of Akkersdijk (field by the dyke)
- Assenberg – a mountainous region with ash trees (*essen*=trees + *berg*=mountain)
- Baars – the town of Beers
- Daalman, Daalmans, Daelman, Daelmans – someone who lived in a valley/dale (*dal*)
- Eikenboom – a place with oak trees (*eik*=oak + *boom*=tree)
- Langbroek – a small town in Utrecht (derived from *lang*=wide + *broek*=swamp)
- Rietveld – a field of reeds (*riet*=reed + *veld*=field)
- Roijackers, Roijakkers, Rooijakkers – a field of reeds (*riet*=reed + *akker*=field)
- Romeijnders – originally from Rome

- Roosevelt – a place near a rose field (*roos*=rose + *velt*=field)

A smaller group of surnames got their names from **physical characteristics, personality traits**, or other descriptors.

- Baart – bearded person
- Coons – bold, daring
- De Groot – the great
- De Jong – the young
- De Wees – the orphan
- De Wit/De With/De Witt/De Witte – the white (a person with white or blond hair)
- Grootaert – someone who is large (suffix *-aert*, meaning *someone who*)
- Krom – bent, crippled
- (De) Lange – (the) tall
- Prinsen – someone who acted in a regal manner (literally, son of a prince)
- Vrooman – wise, valiant, pious man

Surnames that come from **animals** were derived from nicknames that make reference to personality traits typified by those animals.

- De Haas – the hare, nickname for a swift person
- Kikkert – frog
- Vogel – bird, perhaps for a person who likes to sing, or an occupational name for a bird catcher
- Vos – fox, perhaps referring to a sly, cunning individual

The 10 most common Dutch surnames in the Netherlands in 2007 were (Hoitink, 2013b):

1. **De Jong** (the young)
2. **Jansen** (son of John)
3. **De Vries** (the Frisian)
4. **Van de Berg / Van den Berg / Van der Berg** (from the mountain)
5. **Van Dijk / Van Dyk** (from the dyke)
6. **Bakker** (baker)
7. **Janssen** (son of John)
8. **Visser** (fisherman)
9. **Smit** (blacksmith)

10. **Meijer / Meyer** (farmer who represented the landlord of feudal estates)

So now, for a bit of levity, we couldn't end the discussion on Dutch surnames without mentioning some very funny names. It is widely believed that when Napoleon's army occupied the Netherlands and imposed the Napoleonic Code in the beginning of the 19th century, they also forced the Dutch people to adopt surnames and register them for census and tax collecting purposes. Believing this to be a temporary measure, the Dutch protested the order by choosing some pretty hilarious names as practical jokes on their French occupiers. In the end, the joke was on them because they were stuck with those names. However, the Dutch don't seem to find these surnames as humorous as we do, and in fact, they are rather proud of their origin.

- Aarsman (assman)
- Achterop (behind)
- Beddeggenoodts (bedmate)
- Billekes (buttocks)
- Bloot (naked)
- Borst (breast)
- Doodeman (dead man)
- Fijnebuik (nice belly)
- Gekkehuis (madhouse)
- Hoogenboezem (high bosom)
- Komtebedde (come to bed)
- Naaktgeboren (born naked)
- Niemands (nobody)
- Niemantsvrdriet (no man's trouble)
- Niemandsvriend (nobody's friend)
- Onderbroek (underpants)
- Paardebek (horse's mouth)
- Pannenkoek (pancake)
- Piest (he/she pees)
- Poepjes (faeces)
- Rotmensen (rotten people)
- Scheefnek (crooked neck)
- Suikerbuik (sugar belly)
- Uittenbroek (out of the pants)
- Zeldenthuis (seldom home)

- Zondergeld (without money)
- Zonderkop (without head)

And then there are some names that sound particularly funny to English speakers—Fokker (breeder), Kok (cook)—but are perfectly ordinary in the Netherlands (The Netherlands by Numbers, 2013).

GERMAN

Considering the changing borders and political influence of the territory that was present-day Germany prior to 1871, when it became a unified country, as well as after World War I, it is not surprising to find German surnames throughout the bordering countries—not just in German-speaking Austria and Switzerland, but in Poland, Hungary, and France as well.

The earliest German names were just a single name made up of two roots with specific meanings that related to the identity of the person. At some point in the 12th century, as populations grew and the need to differentiate among people with the same name became necessary, people began to be referred to as "**given name** called/known as **second name**". This sort of appellation led to actual surnames sometime in the 14th century. Today, most personal names are made up of at least one, usually two, and sometimes more than two given names and a family name. It should not be assumed that the first given name is the one a person necessarily goes by. When that is not the case and the full name is given, it is customary to underline the preferred given name.

The family name was passed on patrilineally, and traditionally, women adopted their husband's name after marriage. In recent years, the laws have evolved in order to bring gender equality to name choices. Today couples have the options to keep their birth names, combine them into one common surname, or either partner can choose to take on the other's name or hyphenate the two. All children in the family must have the same surname, which can be either parent's or the combined surnames of both parents, but not hyphenated.

Unlike most European countries, where patronymic surnames constitute the largest group, German surnames are derived mostly from occupations. Of the top 100 most common surnames in Germany, 44 are occupational, compared to 21 in France and 7 in Russia (Schochenmaier,

2018). Out of the approximately 850,000 German surnames, the most common surname, Müller, is shared by 700,000 people (Born, 2015). Other surname categories are geographic, descriptive, and patronymic.

Abbreviations used in this section are:

- LG: Low German
- MHG: Middle High German
- OHG: Old High German

Occupational surnames often end in ***-er*** or ***-mann.*** The suffix *-er* usually denotes an agent (someone who performs an action). Many of their meanings have changed over the centuries, but these names reflect the occupations of the ancestors rather than of their bearers today.

- Bauer, Baumann – farmer
- Becker – baker
- Beltz – tanner
- Bergmann – miner
- Färber, Ferber – dyer
- Fischer – fisherman
- Fleischer – butcher
- Geissler, Geißler – goat herder
- Gerber – leather preparer
- Hoffmann – steward, estate manager
- Hüber – farmer
- Jäger – hunter
- Kästner, Kistler – cabinet maker
- Kaufmann – merchant, buyer
- Keller – steward, overseer of household stores and accounts
- Klingemann – weapons smith
- Koch – cook
- Köhler – charcoal maker
- Krämer, Kraemer – grocer, shopkeeper
- Krüger – innkeeper or potter, merchant of glass and pottery
- Lehmann – tenant, vassal
- Maurer – mason
- Meier – mayor, steward, farm administrator
- Metzger – butcher
- Müller – miller
- Pfeiffer – piper

- Pflüger – plowman
- Richter – legal official, judge
- Salzmann – extractor or seller of salt
- Schäfer – shepherd
- Schlösser, Schlosser – locksmith
- Schmidt, Schmid, Schmitt, Schmitz – smith
- Schneider – tailor
- Schröder – carter
- Schultz – sheriff, constable
- Schumacher, Schuhmacher – shoemaker
- Schuster, Schuchardt – cobbler, shoemaker
- Tanzer dancer
- Töpfer, Toepfer – potter
- Wagner, Wägner – wagon driver
- Weber – weaver
- Winkler – grocer
- Ziegler – bricklayer
- Zimmermann – carpenter

Surnames referring to **nobility** may indicate descent from someone who worked for a monarch.

- Fürst – prince
- Graf – count
- Herzog – duke
- Kaiser – emperor
- König, Koenig – king
- Kron – crown (*Krone*)
- Ritter – knight

Geographic surnames can be toponymic (derived from a place name) or topographic (descriptive of a location where an ancestor lived). Some **toponymic** surnames are:

- Achterberg – from the name of several places in Germany and the Netherlands (LG *achter*=behind + *Berg*=mountain, hill)
- Bayer – from Bavaria (*Bayern*)
- Böehm – from Bohemia
- Diefenbach – from a municipality with that name, meaning *deep creek*
- Dresdner – from the city of Dresden in Germany

- Heppenheimer – from the city of Heppenheim in Hesse, Germany
- Ingersleben – from the town of Ingersleben, Germany
- Meisner, Meissner – from the German town of Meissen
- Oppenheimer – from Oppenheim, Germany, possibly meaning *marshy home*
- Sachs – from Saxony (*Sachsen*)
- Schweitzer – from Switzerland
- Sulzbach – town in Saarbrücken, Germany, possibly meaning *salty stream* (*Salz*=salt + *Bach*=stream)
- Waxweiler – from the village with the same name in the Eifel region of Germany

Some topographic names are:

- Acker, Ackermann – someone who lived near a field (MHG *Acker*=field)
- Bach, Bachmann – someone who lived by a stream (MHG *Bach*=stream)
- Beckenbauer – a farmer living by a stream (occupational and topographic)
- Birnbaum – someone who lived near a pear tree
- Brückner – someone who lived near a bridge
- Burkhardt – one who lived in a stronghold or fortress
- Ebner – dweller on a flat piece of land (MHG *Ebene*=plateau)
- Eckstein – from a corner stone (OHG *Ecka* = edge, corner + *Stein*=stone)
- Eichel – person who lived near an oak tree (*Eichel*=acorn)
- Glöckner – person who lived near a bell tower, or an occupational surname for someone who worked there
- Grünberg – someone who lived on or near a forest-covered mountain (*grün*=green + *Berg*=mountain, hill)
- Grünewald – someone who lived near a forest (*grün*=green + *Wald*=forest)
- Holzer, Holzmann – someone who lived in or near the woods or an occupational surname for someone who worked with wood (*Holz*=wood)
- Kappel – person who lived near or worked at a chapel; also occupational (from Late Latin *cappella*)

- Nussbaum – someone who lived near a nut tree (*Nuss*=nut + *Baum*=tree)

Prior to the abolition of the monarchy at the end of World War I, surnames beginning with the preposition *von* (from) distinguished members of the nobility in Germany and Austria (Baron Philipp von Neumann, Karl von Habsburg, Friedrich von Hayek). The original use of this preposition during the Middle Ages and the one in effect through the present day has been as a toponymic indicator. As titles of nobility were abolished after 1918, the only accepted use of *von* was as a toponymic or topographic marker.

- Von Der Ahe – topographic name for someone who lived near a creek (*Ahe*=stream)
- Von Eschen – habitational name for someone from Eschen in Bavaria
- Von Ingersleben – habitational name for someone from the town of Ingersleben

Descriptive surnames may refer to physical characteristics or personality traits.

- Braun – with brown hair or dark complexion
- Dürr – thin
- Fleiss, Fleiß – diligence, assiduity
- Fromm – noble, honorable
- Gross, Groß – big, large
- Hertz – big-hearted
- Hoch, Hochmann – tall
- Jung, Junge – young
- Kahler – bald
- Klein – small
- Kneller – originally a name for a loud, disruptive person
- Kraus, Krause, Krauss – curly
- Kurtz, Kurtzmann – short
- Lang – long
- Riese – giant
- Rot, Roth – red, redhead
- Sauer – sour, a nickname for an embittered or cantankerous person
- Schimmelpfennig – miser

- Schlimme – a bad or crooked person
- Schmeling – slender (*smal*)
- Stark – strong, rigid
- Straub – rough, unkempt
- Sturm – storm, a nickname for a volatile person
- Süß, Süss – sweet
- Teufel – devil, nickname given to a mischievous person
- Weiss – white, nickname for a person with white hair or skin

Many of the surnames derived from animals were nicknames that assigned certain characteristics of that animal to their owners.

- Falk – falcon
- Fuchs – fox (nickname for a redhead)
- Geier – vulture (probably a nickname for a greedy person)
- Hahn – rooster (nickname for a proud, haughty person)
- Kalb – calf
- Maus – mouse (from OHG *Mus*)
- Protz – toad (nickname for a showy, pompous person)
- Rapp – raven (nickname for a person with black hair)
- Reiher – heron (nickname for a person with long legs)
- Specht – woodpecker
- Storch – stork
- Taube – dove
- Vogel – bird (nickname for someone who likes to sing)
- Wolf, Wolff – wolf

Patronymic surnames originating from the given name of the father plus a suffix are most common in Schleswig-Holstein and Ostfriesland in northern Germany, where the Scandinavian influence of these types of names is most prevalent. So Johann the son of Peter was called Johann Petersohn and Johann's son Hans might be called Hans Johannes. These surnames were not hereditary until laws were passed in the late 18th and early 19th centuries that required the adoption of permanent hereditary surnames.

In other areas of Germany, such as Westfalen, Hannover, Lippe-Detmold, Oldenburg and Schlesien, people who owned estate farms often took the farm name (*Hofnamen*) as their surname. Many of these names began or ended in ***-kamp*** or ***-hof***, such as:

- Grasshoff
- Haberkamp
- Kampmeinert
- Kirchhoff
- Neuhof

Many surnames were derived from given names, often made up of two parts, some of which were later shortened. These names have survived even though most of the old German words they were based on are no longer in use.

- Berthold – Berti
- Degenhardt – Gerd
- Günter
- Siegmund – Siggi
- Volkmar – Volker
- Wolfram – Wolf

The 10 most common surnames in Germany are (Forebears, 2012-2022c):

1. **Müller** (miller)
2. **Schmidt** (smith)
3. **Schneider** (tailor)
4. **Fischer** (fisherman)
5. **Weber** (weaver)
6. **Meyer** (manor landlord; later, self-employed farmer)
7. **Wagner** (wainwright)
8. **Becker** (baker)
9. **Schultz** (medieval sheriff)
10. **Hoffmann** (steward)

Other German-speaking countries with traditional German surnames are Austria, Liechtenstein, and the German-speaking cantons of Switzerland. The most common surnames in Luxemburg, which has three official languages (Luxembourgish, French and German), are also German.

SWISS

Switzerland has four national languages: German, French, Italian and Romansch, of which German (Swiss German) is spoken by about two thirds of the population. Not surprisingly, the list of the 10 most common surnames in Switzerland are all German. The French surname Favre, the most common name in Geneva is no. 38 and Bernasconi, the most common surname in the Italian-speaking canton of Ticino, is no. 89 (Alpenwild, n.d.). Müller is by far the most common surname in the German speaking cantons and in all of Switzerland. The following list of the top 10 most common surnames in Switzerland (Forebears, 2012-2022d) is remarkably similar to the corresponding list of German surnames.

1. **Müller** (miller)
2. **Meier** (bailiff)
3. **Schmid** (smith)
4. **Keller** (someone in charge of food and drink, overseer of a household)
5. **Weber** (weaver)
6. **Schneider** (tailor)
7. **Huber** (farmer)
8. **Meyer** (manor landlord, mayor)
9. **Steiner** (stonemason)
10. **Fischer** (fisherman)

AUSTRIAN

Austrians have been regarded historically as ethnic Germans. The ties between the two countries are based on a common language and culture, and on a centuries-long shared history, which are reflected in their naming traditions. Their surnames are very similar to German surnames, the most common being occupational surnames. Toponymic surnames are taken after specific places in Austria (Gruber, Winkler, Steiner). Some surnames display characteristics of local dialects. In some instances, some areas of Austria use diminutive endings ***-erl, -le*** or ***-li.***

The 10 most common surnames in Austria are (Forebears, 2012-2022e):

1. **Gruber** (one who lives in the valley)
2. **Huber** (land-owning farmer)
3. **Bauer** (farmer)
4. **Wagner** (wainwright)
5. **Müler** (miller)
6. **Pichler** (one who lives near a hill)
7. **Steiner** (one who lives in a stony area)
8. **Mayer** (variant of Meier, a bailiff)
9. **Moser** (one who lives on a moor)
10. **Hofer** (steward)

THE BRITISH ISLES

Located off the northwestern coast of Europe, the British Isles consist of two main islands, Great Britain and Ireland, as well as many smaller islands and island groups, including the Hebrides, the Shetland Islands, the Orkney Islands, the Isles of Scilly, and the Isle of Man.

The United Kingdom of Great Britain and Ireland was a sovereign state between 1801 and 1922. After the establishment of the Irish Free State in 1922, the rest of the kingdom was renamed the United Kingdom of Great Britain and Northern Ireland. Great Britain consists of England, Scotland and Wales.

This section examines English, Welsh, Scottish and Irish surname patterns. Because of their common heritage and history, as well as geographic proximity and extensive migration, many surnames are shared by all of them. This is especially true of many Scots and Irish, whose common heritage points to their descent from the indigenous Celtic tribes of Scotland and their Gaelic language.

Abbreviations used in this section are:

- OE: Old English (also known as Anglo-Saxon) – 400s-1066 in England
- ME: Middle English (also known as Anglo-Norman or French Norman) – 1066-1400s in England
- OF: Old French – 8th-14th century in Northern France (later evolved into Middle French)
- OW: Old Welsh – 800-1150 in Wales (later evolved into Middle Welsh)
- ON: Old Norse – 1150-1350 in Scandinavian countries

ENGLISH

Hereditary surnames were first introduced in Britain with the Norman Conquest of 1066. As the population grew, it became necessary to distinguish among people with the same given name by using a byname. This name could describe an occupation or a personal characteristic or personality trait, a physical characteristic of a place of origin, or the given name of one's father. A common way of distinguishing between two men named John, for instance, is by including the name of the father, or rarely, the mother—John Harrison/Harris and John Williamson/Williams. At first, these names changed as people moved from one place to another, changed occupations, or, in the case of patronyms, from one generation to the next.

Most of these names were toponymic, named after their estates, and were usually inherited by the eldest son along with property. They were a symbol of gentle birth and high standing. The first hereditary surname, *de Cantebrigg*, was legally recognized in 1267, but it was not until the 15th century that a majority of the population bore hereditary family names. During this early period, married women either kept their maiden surname or took their husband's name with the suffix *-wif*. The title *Mrs.*

did not come into use until the 16th century. So if Mary Peabody married John Richards, she would be known either as Mary Peabody or as Mary Richardswyf.

Toponymic or **habitational** surnames, derived from the name of a homestead where the original family lived, are a common type of English surname. They might include the name of the town, village, hamlet, county, manor, or estate where they lived or worked. The invading Normans were known by the names of their estates. Many of these places were in Normandy and their names were adapted to the English language. They often began with ***De, Du, De la*** or ***Des*** and ended with ***-aux, -beau, -champ, -court, -eux, -mont, -val, -ville,*** or other French suffixes.

Toponymic surnames of English origin often end in ***-by, -don, -ford, -ham, -ley,*** or ***-ton.***

- Beverley, Beverly – name of city, derived from OE *beofor*=beaver + *licc*=stream
- Bingham – from the town Bingham in Nottinghamshire, possibly derived from OE *bing*=hollow + *ham*=homestead
- Carlisle – city in the county of Cumberland derived from Celtic *cair*=castle, fort + *liwelyd* (pre-Roman personal name *Luguvalos/Luguvalium*)
- Devon, Devons – dweller of the county of Devon
- Hamilton – village in Leicestershire, England
- Huxley – from the name of a village in Cheshire + *leah* (woodland, clearing)
- Johnston – (St.) John's town
- Kent – county in southeast England meaning *border land* (from Celtic *canto*, Welsh *cant*=rim, border)
- Lincoln – city in the county of Lincolnshire, derived from the Roman name *Lindum Colonia*, which evolved to *Lindocolina* (equivalent to the Welsh *llyn*=lake + colony)
- London – the city of London, settled in 43 CE and named Londinium by the Romans
- Middleton – any of many places with this name (from OE *midel*=middle + *tun*=settlement, enclosure)
- Windsor – from any of several English towns (from OE *windels*=windlass + *ora*=bank)

- York – from the city in northern England (original name *Eburacum*=yew tree), or from any town by that name from the county of Yorkshire

An even larger group of surnames are **topographic**, which describe features of the landscape surrounding the homestead of an ancestor. Some toponymic names are derived from topographic features, as seen above.

- Appleby – apple farm (OE *æppel*=apple + ON *býr*=farm, settlement)
- Appleton – orchard (OE *æppel*=apple + *tun*=enclosure, yard)
- Ashley, Ashton – land with ash trees (*æsc*=ash tree + *leah*=clearing or *tun*=yard, town)
- Attenborough – dweller by a fort (from ME *atten*=at the + OE *burg, burh*=fort, fortified place)
- Atwell – by the well
- Atwood, Attwood – near the woods (from ME *dweller at the wood*)
- Barnes – someone who lived near or worked at a barn
- Barton – someone who lived or worked on a barley farm; barley town (OE)
- Brodie – muddy place
- Brooks – someone residing near a stream
- Burton – fort settlement (*burh*=fort + *tun*=settlement, enclosure)
- Bush – someone who lived near a bushy area (from OE *busc* or ON *buskr*)
- Byfield – someone who lived near a patch of open land (from ME *bi*=by, beside + *felde*=open land)
- Field, Fielder – field, pasture (from OE *feld*)
- Ford – someone who lives near a ford
- Forest, Forrest – forest
- Gates, Yates – someone who lived near the town gates
- Green – someone who lived near the village green
- Hall – someone who lived or worked in a hall (house of a medieval noble)
- Haycock, Haycox – from hay mounds or fields (from OE *cock*=mound, field)
- Heath – heath or open field
- Hill – someone who lives on a hill

- Hurst – wooded hill
- Hyde – a parcel of land (about 100 acres)
- Moore – uncultivated land (derived from ME *mor*=open land)
- Perry – pear tree
- Ross – promontory (cognate of Gaelic *ros* or Welsh *rhós*=upland, mooreland)
- Shaw – someone who lived near woods
- Stone – someone who lived in a stony area or worked with stone (from OE *stan*)
- Sykes – marshy stream
- Thorn, Thorne – someone who lived near a thorn bush
- Thorpe – village (from ON *þorp*=hamlet, village)
- Townsend – on the edge of town
- Underhill – at the foot of a hill (from OE *under* + *hyll*=hill)
- Underwood – at the edge of the woods (from OE *under* + *wudu*=woods)
- Wells – well (from ME *wille*=well, spring, water hole)
- West – for someone who lived by the west of a settlement
- Wood – wood, forest (from OE *wudu*)

Occupational surnames were originally also patronymic. They were derived from a person's occupation, trade or position in society, many dating back to medieval times.

- Ackerman, Akerman – ploughman (from ME *aker*=field + *man*)
- Bailey – bailiff (from ME *baili*, via OF from Latin *baiulus*=porter)
- Baker – baker
- Barber – barber
- Barker – tanner
- Bateman – servant of a man named Bate/Bates
- Baxter – lady baker
- Beck – pickaxe (from OE *becca*)
- Brewster – lady brewer
- Butler – wine steward
- Carter – transporter of goods by cart/wagon
- Chapman – seller of goods, shopkeeper, merchant
- Clark, Clarke – clerk, cleric, scribe
- Cook – cook
- Cooper – maker or repairer of wooden containers

- Demsptер – judge (from OE *deemester*)
- Faulkner – keeper of falcons
- Fisher, Fishman – fisherman
- Fletcher – arrow maker
- Forester – keeper of or one in charge of a forest
- Foster – maker of scissors (from OF *forcetier*) or of saddle trees (OF *fustier*); it could also be a derivation of *Forester*
- Fowler – fowler or bird catcher (from OE *fugol*=bird)
- Gardener, Gardiner, Gardner, Garner, Garnier – gardener (from OF *jardin*=garden)
- Garnet, Garnett – hinge maker (from OF *carne*=hinge)
- Glass, Glazier – glass blower or glazier (from OE *glæs*=glass)
- Glover – glove maker or seller
- Graves – steward (from ME *greyve*)
- Harper – harp maker or harp player
- Hickman – servant of a man named Hick
- Hooper – someone who puts metal hoops on wooden barrels
- Hunt, Hunter – hunter
- Inman – inn keeper
- Joiner, Joyner – carpenter, furniture maker (by joining wood pieces together)
- Keen – bold, brave (from OE *cene*)
- Kellogg – pig butcher (from ME *killen*=to kill + *hog*=pig)
- Kitchener – kitchen worker
- Knight – knight (from OE *cniht*)
- Lister – dyer
- Marshall – tender of horses (Norman *mareschal*, from *marah*=horse)
- Smith – smith
- Spencer – dispenser, house steward (from OF)
- Stewart, Steward – hall guardian, warden
- Taylor – tailor
- Turner – maker of objects from wool or metal
- Wainwright – cart maker
- Walker – wool maker (from pounding the wool with their feet)
- Ward – guardian, watchman (from OE)
- Weaver, Webb, Webber, Webster – weaver (from OE)
- Wheeler – wheelwright

- Wright – craftsman, wagon maker (from OE *wrytha*=shaper of wood)

Descriptive surnames are based on a physical characteristic or personality trait, often derived from a nickname or pet name.

- Armstrong – a strong looking person
- Beck – person with a big nose (from ME *beke*=beak)
- Black – person with dark complexion (from OE *blæc*=black) or someone with pale complexion (from OE *blac*=pale)
- Brown – someone with brown hair
- Cole – swarthy, of coal-black complexion
- Cox – little (from OE *cocc*=little); diminutive ending, as in *Wilcox* or *Wilcocks*
- Fox – originally a nickname for a red head or a crafty person
- Graham – grey home (variant of OE *Grahame* or *Graeme*)
- Grant – grand, tall, great (from ME and OF)
- Gray – someone with grey hair or grey clothes
- Green, Greene – someone who often wore green or who lived near the village green
- Hawk – someone who looked or acted like a hawk (from OE)
- Lamb – a kind, gentle person
- Little – someone of short stature
- Lloyd – grey (from OW and ME *llwyd*=grey)
- Moody – brave, bold (OE *modig*)
- Moore – of dark complexion (from OF *more*, from Latin *maurus*=Moorish)
- Payne – rustic, countryman (from OF *paien*, from Latin *paganus*)
- Short – short
- Swift – quick, fast moving (from OE *swift*)
- Tait – cheerful (from ON *teitr*)
- White – someone with white hair or fair complexion
- Wise – wise
- Young – young (from OE *geong*=the young one)

Patronymic/Matronymic surnames were derived from the personal name of a father, or occasionally the mother or another relative, so they used to change with each generation until fixed family names became mandatory. They are formed by adding ***-son*** or the shortened version ***-s*** to the personal name of the parent. The *-son* suffix is more common in northern England, whereas *-s* is preferred in southern and central areas of the country.

The patronymic prefix ***Fitz-*** was introduced into English by the Normans in the 11th century. It is derived from the French word *fils* (*son*). With time, it became a common way to identify illegitimate children of royals, although not exclusively so. It is also found in Irish surnames.

Patronyms/Matronyms*

- Adams, Adamson – offspring of Adam
- Alberts, Albertson – offspring of Albert
- Allison – offspring of Alan or offspring of Alexander
- Anderson, Andrews, Andrewson – offspring of Andrew
- Anson* – offspring of Agnes
- Atkinson, Aitchison – offspring of Atkin
- Christopherson – offspring of Christopher
- Collins – offspring of Colin
- Davidson, Davison, Davies, Davis – offspring of David
- Edison* – offspring of Eda (Edith) or offspring of Eadwig or offspring of Edward
- Edwards, Edwardson – offspring of Edward
- Evanson – offspring of Evan
- Fitzgerald – offspring of Gerald
- Fitzroy – offspring of the king
- Fitzsimmons – offspring of Simon
- Grayson – offspring of Graves, the steward
- Harris, Harrison – offspring of Harry
- Hilliard* – offspring of Hildegard
- Hughes – offspring of Hugh
- Jameson, Jamison – offspring of James
- Jeffers, Jefferson – offspring of Jeffrey
- Johns, Johnson – offspring of John
- Madison* – offspring of Maud, a medieval form of *Matilda*
- Marriott* – offspring of Mary
- Michaels, Michaelson – offspring of Michael
- Mollison* – offspring of Molly
- Morrison – offspring of Morris
- Nelson, Nielson, Niles – offspring of Neil
- Nicholson, Nicolson, Nixon – offspring of Nicholas
- Peters, Peterson – offspring of Peter

- Phelps, Philips, Phillips – offspring of Philip
- Richards, Richardson – offspring of Richard
- Simonson, Simpson – offspring of Simon
- Stephenson, Stevenson – offspring of Stephen
- Tennison, Tennyson – offspring of Denis
- Thompson, Thomson – offspring of Thomas
- Watson – offspring of Walter
- Williams, Williamson – offspring of William

Many surnames are derived from **personal names**. Sometimes a middle name might have been adopted as a surname.

- Adair – from Edgar
- Adam, Adams – from Adam
- Alberts – from Albert
- Allan, Allen – from Alan
- Bennet, Bennett – from Bennett
- Christopher, Christophers – from Christopher
- Clemens, Clement – from Clement
- Ellery – from Hilary
- Garret, Garrett, Garrod – from Gerald
- Gregory – from Gregory
- Hammond – from OF name Hamon
- Harrell – from Harold
- Hendry, Henry – from Henry
- James – from Jacob (Latin form of Hebrew name *Jacob*)
- Jeffery, Jeffries – from Jeffrey
- Jones – from Jon, medieval variant of *John*
- Nichols – from Nichol
- Nigel – from Neil
- Richard, Rickard – from Richard
- Simon, Simons, Simmons, Simpkin, Symonds, Symons – from Simon
- Stephens, Stevens – from Stephen
- William, Willis – from William

Diminutive forms and pet names of given names were popular in the Middle Ages, and with time, many of them formed the basis for surnames. Here is a small sample of the nicknames and some derivations:

- From Adam – Adkin, Adkins, Atkin, Atkins, Atkinson
- From Alan – Alcok
- From Alexander – Sander, Sanders, Sanderson, Saunders
- From Batholomew – Bartlett, Bate, Bates
- From Emma – Emmett
- From Gilbert – Gibbon
- From Hawk – Hawking, Hawkins
- From Hugh – Hewitt, Huchin, Hutchins, Hutchinson
- From Jen (ME for John) – Jenkins, Jennings
- From John – John, Johns, Jack
- From Joseph – Jessel
- From Luke – Lockett
- From Martin – Martel
- From Patrick – Paton
- From Peter – Perkin, Perkins
- From Richard – Dick, Dicks, Dickey, Dicken, Dickens, Dickson, Dickinson, Diggins, Diggens, Dickerson, Dixon
- From Richard – Hicks, Higgs, Ickes, Hickerson, Hicklin, Hicock, Higgens, Hitchcock
- From Robert – Dobbs, Dobson, Dobbins, Dobbison, Dobieson
- From Robert – Hobbs, Hobbes, Hobson, Hopson, Hobkins, Hobkinson, Hopkins, Hopkinson
- From Robert – Nobbs, Nobbes, Nobes, Nopps, Nopkins
- From Roger – Dodgson, Hodgson, Hodges, Hodgens, Hodgkiss, Hotchkins, Hodgins, Hotchkins, Hodkinson
- From Simon – Sim, Sims, Simms
- From Thomas – Tomkin, Thompkins, Thompsett
- From Walter – Watts (ruler of the army, from *wald*=rule + *heri*=army)
- From William – Wilkin, Wilkins, Wilkinson, Wilson, Wilcox, Wilcocks

Ethnic surnames

- English – English (from OE *Englisc*) was originally used to distinguish someone of Anglo descent from a Saxon in the British Isles. In Welsh and Scottish areas bordering England, it usually referred to an Englishman.

- Ireland – Scottish name for a person who lived in Ireland (derivations from the Norman surnames *de Yrlande* and *le Ireis*, designating emigrants from Ireland)
- Scott – Scottish or Gaelic speaking (from OE *scotti*, generic name given by the Romans to Gaelic raiders from Ireland)
- Walsh, Welch – of Welsh or Celtic origin (from OE *welisċ*=foreiger), taken to Ireland by British soldiers during and after the Norman invasion of Ireland

The 20 most common British surnames in 2016 were (Embury-Dennis, 2016):

1. **Smith** (English and Scottish occupational name meaning *blacksmith*, from ME)
2. **Jones** (English and Welsh variant of the ME personal name *Jon*)
3. **Williams** (variant of *William*, a ME personal name)
4. **Taylor** (English surname of French origin from *tailleur*, meaning cutter of cloth)
5. **Davies** (English and Welsh patronymic surname, meaning *the son of David*, introduced after the Crusades)
6. **Brown** (English and Scottish nickname for a person with brown hair or brown complexion)
7. **Wilson** (English patronymic name that means *son of Will*, a shortened form of *William*)
8. **Evans** (variant of *Evan*, a Welsh form of the English name *John*)
9. **Thomas** (English and Welsh name from the New Testament, from Christ's disciple *St. Thomas*)
10. **Johnson** (Anglo-Scottish patronymic name that means *son of John*, derived from the Hebrew name *Yochanan*, meaning *God has favoured me*)
11. **Roberts** (English variant of the ME personal name *Robert*, introduced by the Normans)
12. **Walker** (English and Scottish occupational name for a fuller – someone who beats and presses cloth to make if denser)
13. **Wright** (English and Scottish occupational name from ME for a craftsman, particularly a carpenter or a joiner)
14. **Robinson** (English patronymic name that means *son of Robin*, a diminutive of *Robert*)

15. **Thompson** (English patronymic meaning *son of Tom*; Scottish equivalent is *Thomson*)
16. **White** (ME nickname referring to people with fair hair or a pale complexion)
17. **Hughes** (English and Welsh variant of *Hugh*, derived from the Germanic name *Hugo*)
18. **Edwards** (English variant of *Edward*)
19. **Green** (**ME** name for someone who lived by the village green)
20. **Lewis** (ME given name, derived from the OF personal names *Lewis, Leweis* and *Lowis*)

WELSH

Unlike Scottish and Irish, who share a Gaelic language, the Welsh language (Cymraeg) is a member of the Brythonic branch of the Celtic languages. It, along with English, are the two official languages in Wales today.

Although fixed family names began to be adopted in Wales after the Norman invasion, as in most of Britain, they did not become the norm for many centuries, in some areas as late as the 19th century. Welsh naming traditions before they became permanent were strikingly different from the rest of the United Kingdom. The Welsh took patronymic names, but not derived solely from the father's name, as in other European countries. They followed a Celtic naming system that linked them to a string of six to seven generations of ancestors on their paternal side. Knowing their pedigree that far back was a legal necessity, as it was closely tied to the way the legal system operated in all sorts of judicial matters, including inheriting land.

Welsh names, along with Irish and Highland Scottish names, derive from Gaelic personal names. The Welsh word for *son* is ***mab*** or ***map***, which was shortened to ***ab*** or ***ap***, and the word for *daughter* is ***verch*** (pronounced *ferk*, and shortened to *vch*). A man's first name would be linked by the prefix *ab* or *ap* to his father's first name and likewise to his paternal pedigree several generations back. So Evan the son of Owen's lineage might be recorded as *Evan ap Owain ap Rhys ap Gruffydd ap Hew ap Hywel ap Baughn ap Dafydd*, which, when Anglicized, would be equivalent to *Evan son of Owen son of Rees son of Griffith son of Hugh son* *of Howell son of Vaughn son of David.* When fixed family names were adopted, Evan was free to choose any of his pedigree names, so he could become Evan Owen / Owens / Bowen, Evan Rees, Evan Griffith / Griffiths, etc.

If Owain had a daughter named Enid, her lineage would be recorded as Enid vch Owain ap Rhys ap Gruffydd ap Hew ap Hywel ap Baughn ap Dafydd. She would retain her patronymic name for the rest of her life.

Sometimes *ap* or *ab* was retained, usually in a reduced form, as part of the adopted patronymic (ap Hywel → Powell, ap Rhys → Price, ab Owain → Bowen, ap Richard → Pritchard, ap John → Upjohn, ab Einws → Baines, ab Evan → Bevan). Mostly though, the chosen patronymic gained the suffix *-s* (Roberts, Williams, Griffiths, Jones, Davies, Evans, Hughes). Many Welsh patronymics were derived from given names introduced by the Normans (such as Edward, Henry, Robert, Roger) rather than from truly Welsh names (like Llywelyn, Madog, Rhys).

The Welsh patronymic naming system created the recycling of a small number of given names in a relatively small area. Not surprisingly, this led to a few patronymic surnames belonging to a large percentage of the population, which created a need for further distinction and a trend toward double surnames. These took the form of a first surname representing a place of residence, a mother's surname or another identifying element followed by the actual surname. Sometimes the two were hyphenated (Cynddylan Jones, Rees-Jones, Llewelyn Jones).

The top 10 most common Welsh surnames today constitute 55% of the entire Welsh population (Cooper, 2020).

1. **Jones** (son of John)
2. **Davies** (son of David)
3. **Williams** (son of William)
4. **Evans** (son of Evan)
5. **Thomas** (from given name Thomas)
6. **Roberts** (son of Robert)
7. **Lewis** (Anglicism of Llewelyn, possibly also a patronymic – son of Louis/Lewis)
8. **Hughes** (son of Hugh)
9. **Morgan** (from given name Morcan)
10. **Griffiths** (son of Griffin/Griffith)

The lists below, corresponding to the usual categories of surnames, show the relatively small number of Welsh surnames. The largest groups are patronymic or derivations of personal names. There are very few locational and occupational names.

Patronymic surnames

- Baines – son of Einws, a diminutive of Einion (from Welsh *ab Einws*)
- Bevan, Beavin– son of Evan/John (from *ap Evan, ab Lefan* or *ap Lefan*)
- Bowen – son of Owen (from *ab Owen*)
- Edwards – son of Edward
- Evans – son of Evan
- Griffiths – son of Griffin/Griffith
- Hopkins – son of Hopkin/Hop/Hob, from Robert
- Hughes – son of Hugh
- Jenks, Jenkins – son of Jenk, Jenkin (little John)
- Jones – son of John
- Maneely – son of Neely (from *map Neely*)
- Parry – son of Harry (from *ap Harry*)
- Pierce – son of Piers (from *ap Piers*, Welsh for *Peter*)
- Price, Pryce, Prys, Rees, Rice – son of Rhys (from *ap Rhys*)
- Pritchard – son of Richard (from *ap Richard*)
- Prosser – son of Roger (from *ap Rhosier* or *ap Rosser*)
- Pugh – son of Hugh (from *ap Hugh*)
- Richards – son of Richard
- Roberts – son of Robert
- Rowlands – son of Rowland
- Williams – son of William

Surnames derived from **personal names**

- Cadogan – from Welsh male name Cadwgan (glory in battle, from *cad*=battle + *gwgan*=glory)
- Cecil – from the Welsh given name *Seisyll*, derived from the Roman *Sextilius*, from *Sextus*
- Craddock – from the personal name *Caradoc*, from ancient Celtic name *Caratacos* (*car*=love)
- Davies – from *David*
- Edris – variant of personal name Idris (*udd*=lord + *ris*=ardent)

- Ellis – from personal name *Elisedd*, also patronymic (son of Ellis)
- Gittins – from *Gutyn*, a diminutive of *Gruffudd* (OW *Grifud*)
- Greenway – from given name *Goronwy*
- Griffin, Griffith – from given name *Gruffudd* (OW *Grifud*, from *cryf*=strong + *udd*=lord)
- Kendrick – from OW personal name *Cynwrig* (*cyn*=chief + *gwr*=man)
- Llewelyn, Lewis – from Llewelyn, Llywelyn (from *llyv*=leader)
- Meredith – from personal name *Meredydd/Maredudd*, from OW *Morgetiud*
- Merick, Merriam – from personal name *Meuric*
- Morgan – from OW personal name *Morcan*
- Oliver – from given name *Oliver*
- Owen – from personal name *Owain*
- Roderick – from personal name *Rhydderch* (meaning *reddish-brown*)
- Thomas – from Thomas (*Tomos*, originally from Hebrew *ta'om*=twin)
- Tudor – from Welsh personal name *Tudur* (from OW *Tutir*, from Celtic *Toutorix*=ruler of the people, equivalent to *Theodore,* Greek for *God's gift*)
- Yarwood – from Welsh personal name *Iorwerth* (*ior*=lord + *berth*=handsome)

Toponymic surnames

- Cardiff – from the city of Cardiff (*caer*=fort + *taf*=stream of water)
- Conway – from a fortified town on the North Wales coast, from the river Conwy
- Elwy – from the river Elwy in Wales
- Flint – from the town of Flint in the county of Flintshire
- Kenyon – from Ennion's Mound
- Kerry – near the castle (OW)
- Pembroke – from the town of Pembroke
- Yale – fertile upland (*ial*)

Topographic surnames

- Bryn, Brynn – hill
- Glynn – valley (from *glyn*)

- Trevor – large town (*tref*=town + *mawr*=large)

Descriptive surnames

- Balch – proud, but also fine, splendid, glad, arrogant
- Bledig – like a wolf
- Bragg – cheerful, lively (from ME *bragge*)
- Ellis – kind, benevolent (from personal name *Elisedd*, from *elus*=kind)
- Floyd – variant of Lloyd
- Frost – excessively bold (originally spelled *Ffrost*)
- Gaines – crafty, ingenious (from a reduced form of OF *engaine*=ingenuity, trickery)
- Glace – gray, silver-haired, green (*glas*)
- Goff, Gough – red-haired (from *coch*=red)
- Gwynne (in the south), Wynn, Wynne (in the north) – light, of fair complexion (from *gwyn*)
- Hier – tall, long (from *hir*)
- Lloyd – grey (from *llwyd*)
- Melyn – yellow
- Tew – fat, portly
- Vaughan, Vaughn, Baughan – little, junior (from *bychan*, from *fychan*)

Ocupational surnames

- Gravenor – great hunter
- Melinydd – miller

SCOTTISH

Scottish Gaelic, like the Irish language, is a member of the Goidelic branch of the Celtic language family. In this section, the term Gaelic refers to Scottish Gaelic, to differentiate it from the Irish Gaelic (Gaeilge) spoken in Ireland.

Surnames were first introduced in Scotland by the Normans early in the 12th century; they began to gain popularity around the 16th century, finally spreading to the Highlands and northern isles by the turn of the 19th century. Before this, people were known only by their given name (*forename* in Scotland). Since there was a relatively small set of forenames for parents to choose from, there were a lot of people with the same given name, which necessitated the use of bynames to distinguish among them. These bynames eventually became the fixed, heritable surnames we know today.

The most common Scottish surnames originate from patronymics, descending through the generations from a male ancestor's name or a clan name. Original patronymics were formed differently depending on what part of Scotland they were in. In the Lowlands, they were usually formed by adding the suffix ***-son*** or ***-daughter*** (usually abbreviated in the records as ***-daur***, ***-dr*** or ***-d***) to one's father's given name (Johnson, Thomson, Fergusdaur, Fergusdr). This practice died out after the 15th century, as these types of names became permanent family surnames.

In the Highlands, the more common practice was to add the prefix ***Mac*** or ***Mc*** for boys and ***Nc*** (an abbreviation of *nighean mhic*) for girls to the beginning of the father's forename (Mcarthur, Macneil, Ncdonald, Ncdugall). In earlier records, people were known by their father's and their grandfather's names. The prefix ***Vc*** was used for grandsons and granddaughters. So the birth of a child might have been recorded as *Ean Mcgregor VcDonald, born to Gregor Mcdonald Vcgibbon and Elspeth Ncdugall Vciver*. These practices persisted into the 18th and 19th centuries, when these names became permanent and inheritable surnames.

In the following lists, the original meanings of the names refer to Gaelic/Old Scottish names, unless otherwise noted.

- Acheson, Atchison, Atkinson – offspring of Atkin, medieval diminutive of Adam
- Anderson – offspring of Andrew
- Christie – offspring of Christopher (or Christ bearing)
- Davidson – offspring of David (or beloved son)
- Dickson – offspring of Dick (or brave ruler)
- Donaldson – offspring of Donald
- Ferguson – offspring of Fergus
- Findlay, Findley, Finlay, Finley – Anglicized form of Mac Fhionnlaigh, offspring of Fionnlagh, meaning *white warrior* (from OI *finn*=white, fair + *láech*=warrior)
- Gibson – offspring of Gib
- Gilchrist – offspring of Gille Críst (from *Mac Gille Chrìosd*= offspring of the servant of Christ)
- Henderson, Kendrick (Celtic) – offspring of Henry

- Jamieson – offspring of James
- Lawson – offspring of Laurence
- MacDonald, McDonald, MacDonell, McDonell – offspring of Donald, ruler of the world (from *Mac Dhòmhnaill*, also the name of the Highland clan)
- MacDougall, McDugall – offspring of Dougal (*Dubhghall*=dark stranger)
- MacGregor – offspring of Gregor (*Mac Griogair*), from the Highland clan *Gregor*
- McLean – offspring of the servant of John (*Mac Gille Eòin*)
- Morrison – offspring of Morris
- Paterson – offspring of Patrick
- Robertson – offspring of Robert
- Sanders, Saunders, Mac Alastair, McAlister – offspring of Sander / Alasdair / Alistair (Scottish Gaelic forms of Alexander)
- Thomson, Thompson – offspring of Thomas
- Watson – offspring of Walter
- Wilson – offspring of William

Sometimes a surname was taken directly from **a given name**.

- Alan, Allan, Allen – from Alan
- Greer, Grier – from Gregor
- Hendry – from Henry
- Jones – variant of John
- Lowry – diminutive of Laurence
- Mitchell – from Michael
- Watt – diminutive of early form of Walter

Other categories of surnames—toponymic, topographic, occupational, descriptive, ethnic—were intrinsically patronymic, as the information they carried reflected back to some distant ancestor.

Toponymic surnames were derived from the location of the homestead where one's ancestor dwelt. Often a place name originated from physical features of the land, hence was originally topographic.

- Ainsley – from Annesley in Nottinghamshire or Ansley in Warwickshire
- Argyll, Argyle – from the region of Argyll
- Barclay – from the English town of Berkeley (from OE *beorc*=birch + *leah*=clearing)

- Brodie, Brody – from a place in Moray (from *broth*=ditch, mire)
- Buchanan – from the district of Buchanan in Stirlingshire (from *buth*=house + *chanain*=of the canon)
- Crawford – from the settlement of Crawford in Lanarkshire
- Cunningham – from Cunningham in the Ayrshire district
- Douglas, Douglass – from a town in Lanarkshire, named after a tributary of the River Clyde (from *dubh*=dark +*glais*=water, river)
- Dunsmore – from Dunsmore or Dundemore
- Elgin – from Elgin, in the Moray region
- Gordon – from place in Berwickshire (from Brythonic for *spacious fort*)
- Hamilton – old town in Leicestershire no longer in existence (*hamel*=crooked + *dun*=hill)
- Houston – town near Glasgow meaning *Hugh's town*
- Knox – various places in Scotland and northern England (from *cnoc*=round hill)
- Munroe, Munro – from near the mouth of the Roe River in Derry, Ireland (*bun*=root, base + Roe)
- Murray, Moray – sea settlement in the early kingdom of Moray near the Moray Sea
- Sinclair – of Norman origin, from the old French town of Saint-Clair-sur-Elle in La Manche; also the name of a clan (*Clann na Ceàrda*) from the Scottish Highlands

Topographic names are derived from physical characteristics of the land where one's ancestors once dwelt.

- Abercrombie – mouth of the bendy river
- Blair – a place name derived from Gaelic *blàr*=battlefield
- Boyce, Wood – wood (someone who lives in or near a forest)
- Burns – by a stream (from OE *burna*=stream, spring)
- Cairns – near a cairn
- Carr, Kerr – thicket, marsh (from ON *kjarr)*
- Crawford – (1) near a river crossing (from OE *crawe*=crow + *ford*=river crossing)
- (2) a crossing near a battle site (from *cru*=bloody + *ford*=crossing)
- Glen, Glenn – valley (from *glean*)
- Graham – gravelly homestead (from OE *Grantham*)
- Haig – enclosure, pasture (from Old Irish *haga*, from ON *hagi*)

- Hill – one who resides near a hill
- Innes – island (from *inis*=island, a clan name)
- Kelly – grove (from the Cornish word *coille*=grove)
- Kyle, Kyles – person who lived by a strait (from *caol*= channel, strait)
- Logan – little hollow (*lag*=hollow, pit)
- Muir – one who lived near a moor (from ME *more*=moor, fen, open land); equivalent to the English surname *Moore*
- Shaw – someone who lived by a thicket (from ME *s(c)hage, s(c)hawe,* from OE *sceaga*=dweller by the wood)

Occupational surnames reflected the trade or craft of an ancestor. In some cases, some such names still carried the prefix *Mac* or *Mc* (Macmaster, MacMaster), while others had absorbed them into the new name (Lister, Lester).

- Baird – bard or poet (*bàrd*)
- Barber – barber
- Baxter – baker (from ME *bakstere*)
- Caird – workman in brass, craftsman (from *ceard*=craftsman)
- Clachr – stonemason (from *clachair*)
- Clark, Clarke – clerk or cleric (from Latin *clericus*=cleric, scholar, scribe)
- Gow – smith (from *gobha*)
- Hunter – hunter (from OE *hunta*)
- Laird – lord, landowner
- Lister, Lester – offspring of the arrow maker (*Mac an Fleisdeir*)
- MacEntire, MacIntyre, McEntire, McIntyre, Tyree – offspring of the carpenter (*Mac an tSaoir*)
- MacMaster – offspring of the master or cleric
- Marshall – horse servant (might include farrier, groom, horse doctor)
- Murphy – sea warrior (from *Mac Murchadha*, from *muir*=sea + *cath*=battle)
- Ruskin – tanner (*rusgaire*)
- Smith – blacksmith
- Stewart, Stuart – steward (from *stig-weard*=sty-warden, animal warden)
- Webster, Webber – weaver (from OE *webba*)

- Wright – craftsman (from OE *wrytha* = woodworker; definition later extended to other crafts)

Descriptive surnames are based on a personal characteristic or physical feature of an individual, often developed from a nickname.

- Allan, Allen, Alan, Allanach – fair, handsome
- Arthur – a man strong as a bear (from Welsh *arth*=bear + *ur*=man)
- Brown – brown
- Cameron – crooked nose (from *cam*=crooked + *sròn*=nose)
- Campbell – crooked mouth (from *cam*=crooked + *beul*=mouth))
- Duncan – brown warrior
- Fairbairn – beautiful child (from AS *fair*=lovely + *bearn*=child)
- Kenneth – handsome (from personal name *Coinneach*)
- Mackenzie – comely, good-looking (from *Mac Coinnich*, offspring of *Coinneach*)
- Reid – red, of ruddy complexion (*ruadh*)
- Roy – red-haired (*ruadh*)
- Young – young, youthful

A few surnames indicate membership in an **ethnic** group. Not surprisingly, they refer to people originating in neighboring countries.

- Irish – Irishman (also an English name)
- Scott – Scotsman
- Wallace, Wallis – Welsh, Briton, foreigner (from Norman French *waleis*)

According to the National Records of Scotland (2020), the 10 most common names in Scotland in 2020 were:

1. **Smith** (blacksmith)
2. **Brown** (brown)
3. **Wilson** (offspring of William)
4. **Thomson** (offspring of Thomas)
5. **Stewart** (steward)
6. **Robertson** (offspring of Robert)
7. **Campbell** (crooked mouth)
8. **Anderson** (offspring of Andrew)
9. **Scott** (Scotsman)
10. **Taylor** (tailor)

Irish

The Irish (Gaeilge) language, sometimes called Goidelic (from the Old Irish *Goídel*=Irisman) or Gaelic, is a branch of the Celtic language family. It was the first language of the Irish people through the 18th century and is still widely spoken today. In this section, the word Gaelic refers to Irish Gaelic, to differentiate it from the Scottish Gaelic spoken in Scotland.

Family names developed in Ireland as early as the 10th century, making them among Europe's oldest. The first recorded surname was *ó Cléirigh*, derived from the word *cléireach*, meaning *clerk* or *cleric*. Unlike in the rest of Europe, where surnames could be locational, occupational, descriptive, as well as patronymic, most Irish surnames were almost exclusively patronymic due to the organization of medieval Irish society around the extended family. A patronymic surname represented clan membership and affected many areas of daily life.

Patronymic surnames could be formed by prefixing ***Mac*** or ***Mag*** (son) or ***Ó*** or ***Ua*** (grandson) to the genitive case of the father's given name. This could be a native Irish name, such as:

- Mac Aodhagáin (son of Aodhagán)
- Mac Cárthaigh (son of Cárthach)
- Mag Uidhir (son of Odhar)
- Ó Briain (grandson/descendant of Brian)
- Ó hAodha (grandson/descendant of Aodh)
- Ó Néill (grandson/descendant of Niall)

It could also be a name of foreign origin, most likely Norse or Norman.

- Mac Fheórais (son of Piers)
- Mac Íomhair (son of Ivor)
- Mac Maghnuis (son of Magnus)
- Mac Sheóinín (son of little John)
- Ó Bruadair (grandson/descendant of Bruadar)
- Ó Dubhghaill (grandson/descendant of Dubhghaill)
- Ó hArailt (grandson/descendant of Harald)

These prefixes could also be added to the genitive case of a word referring to the trade or occupation of an ancestor of either Irish or foreign origin.

- Mac an Bháird (son of the bard)
- Mac an Ridire (son of the knight)
- Mac an tSaoir (son of the craftsman)
- Ó Gobhann (grandson/descendant of the smith)
- Ó hÍceadha (grandson/descendant of the healer)

Female surnames used a different set of prefixes. The male *Mac* was replaced by ***Nic***, reduced from *Iníon Mhic* (daughter of the son of), and the male *Ó* was replaced by ***Ní***, reduced from *Iníon Uí* (daughter of descendant of). A married woman had the option of keeping her birth name or taking her husband's, in which case *Mac* was replaced by ***Bean Mhic*** (wife of the son of) or simply ***Mhic***, and *Ó* was replaced by ***Bean Uí*** (wife of descendant of) or simply ***Uí***. When Anglicized, female surnames used the same patterns as the male surnames.

Many of the surnames prefixed by *Ó* have been Anglicized and simplified by either a change in vowel (Ó hEachthighearna → Ahearn), by the elision of the prefix (Ó Baoighill → Boyle, Ó Seachnasaigh → O'Shaughnessy/Shaughnessy, Ó Séaghdha → O'Shea/Shea) or, rarely, by its incorporation into the body of the surname (Ó Gnímh → O'Gneeve → Agnew).

Many surnames prefixed by *Mac* have been reduced to *Mc*, omitted, or incorporated into the name (MacRiada → Macready, MacRiaraidhe → Macreary). This incorporation was more common in northern areas, especially when the ancestral name began with a vowel. In this case, the voiceless stop /k/ (letter *c*) in *Mac* became the voiced /*g*/ when surrounded by vowels, a common phonological process known as assimilation. This gave rise to surnames such as Magee (Mac Aodha → Mag Aodha → McGee) and Maguire (Mac Uidhir → Mag Uidhir → McGuire). The further deletion of the initial *Ma-* led to surnames such as Gee, Glynn, Gough and Guinness.

In the 17th century, many dropped the *Mac* and *Ó* prefixes because of anti-Irish sentiment in the workplace, but some families reclaimed them two centuries later.

Some Norman families Hibernicized their names (Dalatún → Dalton, Réamonn → Redmond) or replaced the Norman patronymic prefix *Fitz* by *Mac* (FitzGerald → Mac Gearailt; FitzSimon → Mac Siomúin).

The less common prefix ***Gil-***, from *giolla*, meaning *servant* or *follower*, was usually associated with religious figures.

- Gilchrist – servant of Christ (from *Giolla-Chríost*)
- Gildea – son of the servant of God (from *Mac Giolla Dhé*)
- Gilmore – servant of the Virgin Mary (from *Mac Giolla Mhuire*)
- Gilfoyle – servant of St. Paul (from *Giolla-Phóil*)
- Gilpatrick → Fitzpatrick – follower of St. Patrick (from *Giolla-Pádraic*)
- Gilroy – son of the king's servant (from *Mac Giolla Rí*)

Most Irish surnames were Anglicized in the second half of the 16th century, but the process continued over the next centuries. It was accomplished in several ways (Woulfe, 1923):

1. Phonetically, by writing down names following the English phonetic system without regard to the original Irish spelling. The same Irish surname can give rise to several different surnames and vice versa, different Irish surnames can have the same Anglicized form.

    - Ó Briain → O'Brien
    - Ó Cathbhadha, Ó Cathmhogha, Ó Cobhthaigh → Coffey
    - Ó Ceallacháin → O'Callaghan
    - Ó Dubhthaigh → Duffy, Dowie, Dooley
    - Ó Murchu → Murphy

2. By translating, often incorrectly, the original meaning to English
    - Mac an tSaoir → Freeman, Carpenter
    - Mac Conraoi → King
    - Mac Seáin → Johnson
    - Ó Bruacháin → Banks
    - Ó Draighneáin → Thornton
    - Ó Gaoithín → Wyndham

3. By absorbing an already Anglicized surname into a more common surname of similar sound in the same region.
    - Ó Braoin → O'Breen, Breen → O'Brien
    - Ó Duibhdhíorma → O'Dughierma, Dooyearma → MacDermott
    - Ó Maoil Sheachlainn → O'Melaghlin → MacLoughlin

4. By substituting Irish names for better-sounding and thus, more acceptable names, something the people themselves were eager to do. Sometimes the new names were somewhat similar to the original names.
   - Ó Bruadair → Broderick
   - Ó Buachalla → Buckley
   - Ó Caireallàin → Carlton
   - Ó hAarrachtáin → Harrington

Other times they bore little to no resemblance to the original Irish names.

- Ó Beargha → Barry
- Ó Clúmháin → Clifford
- Ó Fiannachta → Fenton
- Ó Niadh → Neville

In contrast to English naming practices, Irish surnames are never derived from place names. Many are **descriptive.** Although most of them are no longer overtly patronymic after having lost the patronymic suffix, they remain so intrinsically, referring to a physical characteristic or personality trait of an ancestor. The original Gaelic/Old Irish name is given in parentheses.

- Brady – spirited, roguish (from *Ó Brádaigh*, descendant of *Brádach*)
- Casey – vigilant, watchful (from *Ó Cathasaigh*, descendant of *Cathasach*)
- Connelly, Connolly – valiant (from *Ó Conghalaigh*, descendant of *Conghalach*)
- Dempsey – proud (from *Ó Díomasaigh*, descendant of *Díomasach*)
- Devlin – unlucky (from *Ó Doibhilin*, from Gaelic *dobhail*)
- Donnelly, Donnally – valiant dark man (from Ó Donnghaile, descendant of Donnghaile, or Donnghal, whose name is composed of *donn*=brown + *gal*=valor)
- Doyle, McDowell – dark stranger (from *Ó Dubhghaill*, descendant of Dubhgall, a 13th century leader whose personal name was composed of *dubh*=black + *gall*=stranger). Irish equivalents of Scottish *McDougall*

- Duffy – dark, swarthy (from *Ó Dubhthaigh,* descendant of Dubhthach, from *dubh*=black)
- Dunn, Dunne – brown-haired, dark (from *Ó Duinn/Ó Doinn,* descendant of *Donn*)
- Farrell – valiant, brave (from *Ó Fearghail,* descendant of *Fearghal,* whose name is composed of *fer*=man + *gal*=valor)
- Finn, Finnegan – fair, white (from *Old Irish finn)*
- Flynn – red, ruddy (from *Ó Floinn,* descendant of *Flann*)
- Flanagan, Flannagan, Flanagin – scarlet (from *Ó Flannagáin,* descendant of *Flannagán,* from *flann*=scarlet, ruddy)
- Gallagher – lover or helper of foreigners (from *Gallchobhair, gall*=stranger + *cabhair*=help)
- Hagan, Hogan – young (from *Ó hÓgáin,* descendant of *Ógán,* from *óg*=young)
- Keefe, O'Keefe – gentle, dear (from *Ó Caoimh,* descendant of *Caomh*)
- Kennedy – ugly head or helmeted chief or leader (from *Ó Ceanneidigh,* descendant of *Ceannéidigh,* from Gaelic *cean*=head or chief *+éidigh*=ugly). Ceannéidigh, a variation of Cinnéidigh, could also be translated as *helmeted head* or *helmeted chief.*
- Kenny, Kenney – fiery (from the Gaelic family names *Ó Cionaoith* and *O Coinne,* from *cion*=love, affection + *aodh*=the god of fire)
- McCarthy – loving (from *Mac Carthaigh*)
- Moore – majestic (from *Ó Mordha*)
- Moran – great (from *Ó Móráin,* descendant of *Mórán*)
- Mullan – bald (from *Ó Maoláin,* perhaps in reference to the holy monks of ancient Ireland, who had their heads shaved)
- Nolan, Knowland – famous, noble (from *Ó Nualláin,* descendant of *Nuallán,* from *nuall*=famous, loud)
- O'Brien – noble (from *Ó Briain,* descendant of Brian Boru, High King of Ireland)
- O'Doherty, Doherty – hurtful, unlucky (from *Ó Dochartaigh,* descendant of *Dochartach*)
- O'Dwyer, Dwyer – black, dark-colored (from *Ó Dubhuir,* from *dubh*=black, dark + *odhar*=brown)
- O'Sullivan – dark-eyed (from *Ó Súilleabháin,* descendant of *Súileabhán,* from *súildhubhán, súl*=eye + *dubh*=black)

- Quinn – wise, intelligent (from *Ó Cuinn*, descendant of a Gaelic chief *Conn*)
- Sheehan – peaceful (from Ó Síocháin)

Some surnames describe the **title** or **occupation** of an ancestor.

- Buckley – cowherd (from Ó Buachalla, from *buachaill* = herdsman); the equivalent English surname is believed to be habitational.
- Clarke, Cleary, O'Cleary – clergyman (from *Ó Cléirigh*, descendant of *Cléireach*, meaning *clerk* or *cleric*, possibly derived from Latin *clericus*)
- Connery, Conroy – hound keeper (from *Ó Conaire*, descendant of *Conaire*=hound keeper)
- Fallon – leader (from *Ó Fallamhain*, descendant of *Fallamhan*=leader)
- Foley – robber (from *Ó Foghlú*, from *foghlaí*=robber)
- Kearney – warrior (from *Ó Ceithearnaigh*, descendant of *Ceithearnch*=warrior)
- Kelly, O'Kelly – warrior, fighter (*Ó Ceallaigh*, descendant of *Ceallach*, a great Irish chieftain or fighter
- Lynch – seafarer (from *Ó Loinsigh*)
- Murphy – sea warrior (a variant of *Ua Murchadha, Ó* Murchadh, *Mac Murchaidh*, very old Irish surnames that indicate descent from sea warriors, from *muir*=sea + *cath*=battle)
- Murray – lord, master (from *Ó Muireadhaigh*)
- Reagan, Regan, Ryan – little king (from *Ó Riagháin or O'Riain, descendant of Riaghán or Rian,* from *ri*=king + *in*=little)
- Smith – blacksmith, Anglicized equivalent of *Mac an Ghabhain* (MacGowan)

A small number of surnames are derived from names of ancestors that denote an **animal**.

- Byrne, Burns – raven (from *Ó Broin, descendant of Bran*=raven)
- Collins, Cullen – puppy (from *Ó Coileáin*, descendant of *Coileán*=puppy, young dog)
- Connell – rule of a wolf (from *Ó Conaill*, descendant of *Conall*, from *con*, genitive form of *cú*=hound, wolf + *fal*=rule)
- MacMahon, Mahon – bear calf (from *Mac Mathghamhna*, son of *Mathgamain*, from *math*=bear + *gamuin*=calf)

- O'Leary – calf herder (from *Laoghaire/Lóegaire*, from Old Irish *lóeg*=calf)
- Whalen, Whelan, Phelan – little wolf (from *Ó Faoláin*, descendant of *Faolán*)

Other common Irish surnames not included in these categories are:

- Bradley – broad meadow (from *Ó Brolacháin*, descendant of someone who lived near a broad meadow)
- Gallagher – helper of foreigners (from *Ó Gallchobhair*, descendant of *Gallchobhar*, *gall*=strange, foreign + *cabhair*=help, support)
- Hayes, Hughes – fire (from *Ó hAodha*=descendant of *Aodh*, the mythical god of the underworld)
- Heffernan – little demon (from *Ó hIfearnáin*, descendant of *Ifearnán*)
- Monahan, Monaghan – descendant of the little monk (from *Ó Manachain*, from *manach*=monk + *án*=diminutive suffix)
- O'Neill – descendant of the warrior king Niall
- Walsh – Welshman (from *Breathnach*=Briton, used to denote the Welshmen who arrived in Ireland in the wake of the Anglo-Norman invasion of 1170)

The 10 most common surnames in Ireland in 2021 are (Irish Central, 2021):

1. **Murphy** (sea warrior)
2. **Kelly** (fighter, warrior)
3. **O'Brien** (nobleman)
4. **Ryan** (little king)
5. **Byrne** (raven)
6. **O'Connor** (patron of warriors)
7. **Walsh** (Welshman)
8. **O'Sullivan** (dark-eyed)
9. **McCarthy** (loving)
10. **Doyle** (dark stranger)

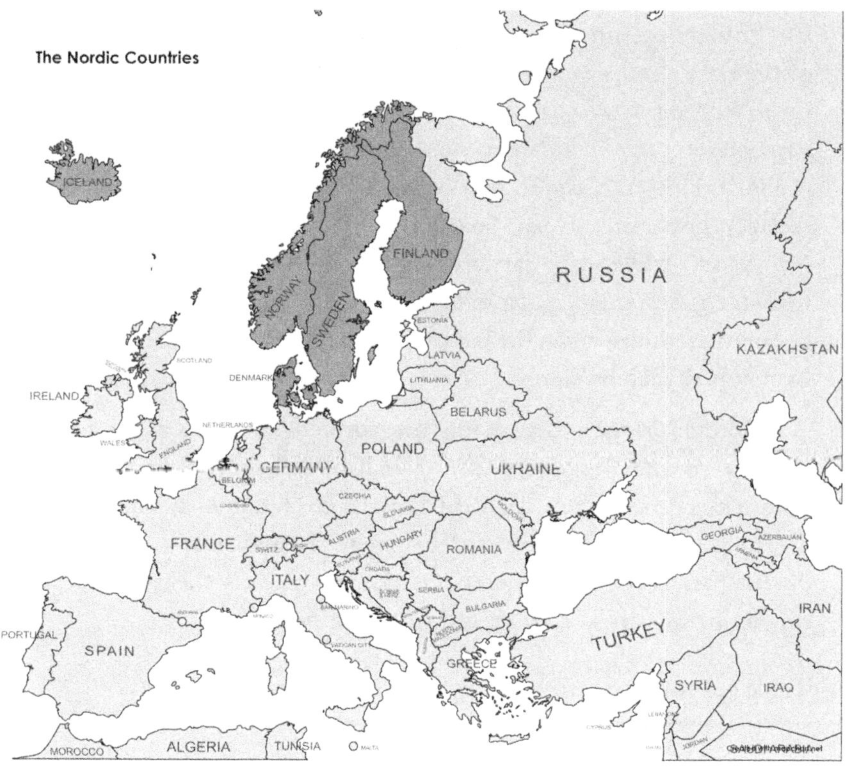

The Nordic Countries

The Nordic countries include Iceland, Denmark, Norway, Sweden and Finland, as well as Greenland, the Faroe Islands and the Åland Islands. Culturally speaking, these countries are also considered to be Scandinavian because of their shared histories, traditions, and political systems. In strict geographic terms, only Denmark, Norway and Sweden are considered Scandinavian countries (Norman, n.d.). Linguistically, however, Danish, Norwegian, Swedish and Icelandic are Scandinavian languages belonging to the Northern Germanic branch of Indo-European languages. Finnish, along with Estonian and Hungarian, belongs to the Finno-Ugric branch of the Uralic language family, and is therefore not an Indo-European language. Surname patterns in the Nordic countries reflect these differences and similarities.

Primary patronyms, which were derived directly from the given name of the father and were not hereditary, were used in the Nordic countries until naming laws forbade their usage, when the use of hereditary surnames became mandatory—in Denmark in 1828, in Sweden in 1901, in Finland in 1921, and in Norway in 1923 (Ancestral Findings, n.d.). In Iceland, however, primary patronyms have been and continue to be mandatory, while secondary patronyms and other types of surnames are forbidden. Secondary patronyms are 'frozen' primary patronyms which became hereditary when the laws mandated them. They were first adopted by nobility, then by clergy, artisans, and merchants who lived in cities.

Nordic primary patronyms are formed by adding the following suffixes to the genitive form (Swedish and Norwegian) or to the nominative form (Danish) of the father's given name, as shown in Table 4. The genitive suffix *-s* precedes the patronymic suffix in Swedish and Norwegian surnames (although it is often dropped in the latter), hence the predominance of ***-ssen, -sson,*** and ***-ssøn*** endings.

Table 4. Primary patronymic suffixes in the Nordic countries

Language	Suffix for 'son'	Suffix for 'daughter'
Icelandic	-son	-dóttir
Danish	-sen	-datter
Norwegian	-sen/-son/-søn	-datter/-dotter
Swedish	-son	-dotter
Finnish	-poika	-tytär

Occasionally, as when the father is unknown, primary matronyms were used by adding the same suffixes to the mother's given name.

The Finnish suffixes seem drastically different from the others, but that is only because Finnish is a non-Indo-European language. The surnames themselves follow similar patterns to those of the Scandinavian countries.

Before the adoption of mandatory surnames, men and women kept their full birth names upon marriage. By the end of the 19th century or beginning of the 20th (depending on the country), when most families were adopting permanent surnames, many women opted to take their husband's surname. Today, many women keep their family name upon marriage or use a double surname (their own followed by their husband's).

ICELANDIC

Unlike the other Nordic countries, Iceland does not have a formal surname system. Icelanders don't have fixed family names that are passed on from one generation to the next.

A small percentage of Icelanders, mainly those who had lived abroad, began to adopt family names in the second half of the 19th century. In 1913, the supreme national parliament of Iceland (the Alþingi) legalized the adoption of family names only to outlaw them in 1925. Those who had family names tended to be government officials or members of the upper class.

The rationale behind the banning of family names was supported by arguments that they were not authentically Icelandic, that surnames ending in *-son* could be confused with true patronymics, or that members of the lower classes would be free to adopt names of upper-class families. On the other hand, proponents of surname adoption argued that fixed family names would make it easier to trace lineages and to distinguish among many individuals with the same patronymic, and they thought Iceland should adopt surnames like the rest of the Nordic countries.

Although Iceland shares a common cultural and linguistic heritage with the other Scandinavian countries, it is the only one that has maintained the traditional patronymic naming system that had once been common to all of them and to the rest of the European countries. With few exceptions, this patronym consists of the genitive form (ending in *-s*) of the first name of the father, or occasionally of the mother, followed by the suffix ***-son*** for males and ***-dóttir*** for females. The neutral suffix ***-bur*** (offspring) was introduced in Iceland in 2019 for people who are officially registered with non-binary gender. Some of the most common Icelandic patronyms are (Carter, n.d.):

- **Árnason** or **Árnadóttir** (offspring of Árni)
- **Björnsson** or **Björnsdóttir** (offspring of Björn)
- **Einarsson** or **Einarsdóttir** (offspring of Einar)
- **Guðmundsson** or **Guðmundsdóttir** (offspring of Guðmundur)
- **Jóhannsson** or **Jóhannsdóttir** (offspring of Jóhann)
- **Jónsson** or **Jónsdóttir** (offspring of Jón)
- **Kristjánsson** or **Kristjánsdóttir** (offspring of Kristján)
- **Magnússon** or **Magnúsdóttir** (offspring of Magnús)
- **Ólafsson** or **Ólafsdóttir** (offspring of Ólaf)
- **Sigurðsson** or **Sigurðardóttir** (offspring of Sigurður)

The popularity of these names depends on the popularity of the given names they are derived from at the time the children were born. Sometimes, if a parent has two given names, the child's patronym may be derived from the second name, either because the parent prefers it or it fits better with the child's given name.

Compared to other nationalities, Icelanders are much more informal in their communication. Using honorifics is extremely rare, even when talking about or to teachers, doctors, political leaders or their elders. First names are used in most situations. Icelanders never use the equivalents of Mr. (*herr/hr.*) Jónsson or Ms. (*frú*) Jónsdóttir. To them, a person's last name is forever connected to the name of the parent.

Everyday life in Iceland is organized on the basis of first names (Hauksdóttir, 2016). School rosters, phone books, and all official and unofficial documents are arranged alphabetically according to first names. When talking about two people with the same given name, their second given name or the patronymic may be added to distinguish between them. Usually, the suffix *-son* or *-dóttir* would be omitted. So, for example, when talking about Jón Stefán Einarsson and Jón Árni Magnússon, their friends would probably refer to them as Jón Stefán and Jón Árni, or as Jón Einars and Jón Magnús.

People live their whole lives with the names they were given at birth. Icelanders who live abroad and adopt a spouse's name upon marriage must use their Icelandic name when returning to Iceland.

The 10 most common surnames in Iceland as of 2017 are Germanic names, but, not surprisingly, there is not a single Icelandic patronymic among them (Statistics Iceland, 2018). After all, they are not considered surnames. The top two names are indeed Icelandic, but their use conforms to the Icelandic naming system by occurring in conjunction with a first name and a patronym (Magnús Blöndahl Sighvatsson, Hjörtur Haraldsson Blöndal, Vigfús Þórarinsson Thorarensen). Contrast these with the previous list of the most common Icelandic patronyms.

1. **Blöndahl** (Icelandic)
2. **Thorarensen** (Icelandic)
3. **Hansen** (Scandinavian)
4. **Olsen** (Scandinavian)
5. **Andersen** (Danish, Norwegian)
6. **Thoroddsen** (Iccelandic)
7. **Möller** (Swedish, German)
8. **Nielsen** (Danish)
9. **Waage** (Norwegian)

DANISH

Denmark was the first Nordic country to abandon the use of primary patronyms, with nobility required to do so by royal decree in 1526. This custom was later extended to clergy and merchants, and by a 1771 decree to most of the Duchy of Schleswig (Fryxell, n.d.). Due to the geographic proximity to Germany, naming customs had been influenced by German surname patterns as early as the Middle Ages. By the time hereditary surnames became mandatory for everyone in 1828, many Danes had already adopted surnames modeled after German patterns—occupational or geographic. Those who hadn't often chose to 'freeze' their primary patronymic names, which then became hereditary. However, it took several decades, until about 1870, before primary patronyms ceased to be used. Due to the importance of agriculture in Denmark, many people took a farm name as either a replacement of or in addition to this new hereditary surname.

Since most people chose their patronymic as their heritable surname, the result was an overwhelming dominance of a few surnames. More than two thirds of Danish surnames end in the patronymic suffix ***-sen***. The 10 most common surnames belong to approximately one third of the Danish population. In order to avoid confusion among people with the same surname, many Danes started using their mothers' birth surnames as a heritable middle name similar to the Russian and Hispanic systems.

However, unlike these systems, this matronymic middle name is not considered an official part of the surname unless it is hyphenated into one compound name.

The Danish existential philosopher Søren Kierkegaard was the son of Ane Sørensdatter Lund Kierkegaard and Michael Pedersen Kierkegaard. We can infer that Kierkegaard was named after his maternal grandfather, Søren, and that his paternal grandfather was named Peder. His mother's maiden name, Lund, is a topographic name referring to an ancestor who lived by a grove, and his and his father's surname means 'church yard'.

The 20 most common Danish surnames as of January 2015 are (Statista, 2022a):

1. **Nielsen** (son of Niels, or Nicholas)
2. **Jensen** (son of Jens, variant of Johannes, or John)
3. **Hansen** (son of Hans, a nickname of Johannes)
4. **Andersen** (son of Anders, or Andrew)
5. **Pedersen** (son of Peder, or Peter)
6. **Christensen** (son of Christen, a variant of Christian)
7. **Larsen** (son of Lars, short for Laurentius, or Lawrence)
8. **Sørensen** (son of Søren)
9. **Rasmussen** (son of Rasmus, short for Erasmus)
10. **Jørgensen** (son of Jørgen, or George)
11. **Petersen** (son of Peter; variation of Pedersen)
12. **Madsen** (son of Mads, nickname of Mathias, or Matthew)
13. **Kristensen** (son of Kristen; variation of Christensen)
14. **Olsen** (son of Ole/Olaf/Olav)
15. **Thomsen** (son of Tom/Thomas)
16. **Christiansen** (son of Christian; variation of Christensen)
17. **Poulsen** (son of Poul, or Paul)
18. **Johansen** (son of Johan)
19. **Møller** (occupational name for 'miller', the most common non-patronymic surname)
20. **Mortensen** (son of Morten)

As we can see, 19 out of the 20 most common Danish surnames are patronymic. Other much smaller categories of surnames are topographic, habitational (taken from farm names or other place names), occupational, and descriptive.

Topographic surnames are derived from forms and features of land surfaces.

- Beck – stream
- Buske – bush
- Colding/Kolding – cold river (a fjord in Denmark)
- Dahl – valley
- Egeberg – mountain of oak trees (*ege*=oak, *berg*=mountain /hill)
- Holm – small island (from Old Norse *holmr*)
- Holt – forest
- Kjaer – marshy areas of low, wet lands
- Koppel – pasture
- Lind – linden tree
- Lund – grove (from Old Norse *lundr*); also a toponymic for someone from Lund, Sweden
- Nordskov – north woods
- Skov – forest, wood
- Strand – beach, sea shore
- Strøm – stream
- Vang/Wang – meadow, grassy slope

Habitational surnames indicate where a person originated at the time surnames were becoming hereditary. They can be derived from towns, villages, manors or farmsteads. The following is a list of habitational surnames derived from farm names:

- Agard – farm by a stream
- Norgaard – north farm (*nord*=north, *gård*=farm)
- Østergaard – eastern farm or east of the farm (*øster*=eastern, *gård*=farm)
- Skovgaard – farm near forest (*skov*=forest, *gård*=farm)
- Søndergaard – southern farm (*sønder*=southern, *gård*=farm)
- Vestergaard – western farm or west of the farm (*vester*=western, *gård*=farm)

The following is a list of habitational surnames derived from towns and villages (toponymic or geographical):

- Dastrup – from any of the Danish villages by that name (*rup, strup, torp, drup* are old Scandinavian terms for a group of houses)
- Faaborg – from the old port town by that name on the Faaborg fjord

- Riber – from Ribe, a Danish town
- Thorup/Torup – from any of such named villages and towns in Denmark
- Tranbarger – from Tranebjerg, Denmark
- Wivell – from the Danish town of Vivild

By comparison to most European surnames, **occupational** surnames are much less common.

- Fisker – fisherman
- Fogt – bailiff, sheriff
- Gram – farmer (derivation of *gran*=grain)
- Horn – someone who carves objects out of horn or a horn player
- Kaas – cheese maker (*kaas*=cheese)
- Kaysen – descendant of a cattle rearer (*kalfr*=calf in Old Norse)
- Møller – miller
- Schmidt – blacksmith

An even smaller group of names are **descriptive** of physical characteristics or personality traits of an ancestor.

- Helt – hero
- Hertz – brave, big-hearted (from Middle High German)
- Lykke – happy, cheerful

Norwegian

The most common Norwegian surnames today come from patronyms, and occasionally, from matronyms. Primary patronyms ended in ***-sen, -son***, or ***-søn*** for males and ***-datter*** or ***-dotter*** for females. Before the 1900s, most names consisted of a given name, a patronym and a farm name. Since there were relatively few common masculine given names, the corresponding patronyms were held by a large number of people, so in order to distibguish among them, a third name—a farm name—was used. Just like in other Nordic countries, hereditary surnames had been used in Norway for several centuries, but they were mostly limited to the educated upper class, which included the clergy, the military, and high ranking civil servants. Many of these names were quite old and were often British, Dutch, or German.

In 1923, Norway was the last of the Nordic countries to mandate the use of hereditary names. However, because of the strong connection to Denmark over the centuries (the two countries formed a union, the Dano-Norwegian Realm, that lasted until 1814), the gradual change toward the adoption of hereditary names began to happen much earlier. Also, industrialization and the migration flows to cities contributed for the need for permanent family names. The Family Name Act of 1923 dictated that the only legal surnames were those obtained through marriage or through blood (FamilySearch, 2022). Children would have the father's surname if the parents were married or the mother's if not. Women would take their husband's surname upon marriage. It wasn't until 1965 that women could again keep their name, men could choose to take their wife's name, and children could use either parent's or both parents' surnames, one as a middle name.

At the end of the 19th century, half of city dwellers had a patronymic surname. In 1923, many Norwegians who had not yet taken a hereditary name chose to adopt their primary patronyms as their family name, but some chose to adopt a farm name. By 2012, 22.4% of the population bore the patronymic surname *-sen*, which is the dominant one of the three original endings, while only 18.4% of children born in 2009 do. And yet, there are 16 names ending in *-sen* among the top 20 most common surnames in Norway today. These are the patronymics based on the most common male given names. The 20 most common surnames in Norway as of 2019 are (Rasin, 2020):

1. **Hansen** (son of Hans)
2. **Johansen** (son of Johan)
3. **Olsen** (son of Ole/Olaf/Olav)
4. **Larsen** (son of Lars)
5. **Andersen** (son of Anders)
6. **Pedersen** (son of Peder)
7. **Nilsen** (son of Nils)
8. **Kristiansen** (son of Kristian)
9. **Jensen** (son of Jens)
10. **Karlsen** (son of Karl)
11. **Johnsen** (son of John)
12. **Pettersen** (son of Petter)
13. **Eriksen** (son of Erik)

14. **Berg** (mountain)
15. **Haugen** (a farm name)
16. **Hagen** (a farm name)
17. **Johannessen** (son of Johannes)
18. **Andreassen** (son of Andreas)
19. **Dahl** (valley)
20. **Jørgensen** (son of Jørgen)

A large number of surnames today originate from farm names, which used to be one part of the three-name identification of people prior to the 20th century. It helped to differentiate between Hans Eriksen Blomhaugen (who lived on the farm of Blomhaugen) from Hans Eriksen Bakken (who lived on the farm called Bakken). The farm names were part of their name as long as they remained on that farm, but changed if they moved to a different one. When hereditary surnames became mandatory, some people chose the name of their farm or of another place (habitational), or a geographical feature of such a place (topographic) as a family name.

The following is a list of **habitational** and/or **topographic** surnames under one category because many of the farm names are derived from topographic features.

- Aaberg/Åberg – a hilly place near a river (*å*=river, stream + *berg*=hill, mountain)
- Berg – mountain
- Bjørklund – a farm meaning 'birch grove' (*bjørk*=birch + *lund*=grove)
- Bøen – common farm name (from ON *býr*=farm, village, settlement)
- Borgedalen – from a fortification in a valley (*borg*=castle + fortification; *dal*=valley)
- Brekke – hill, slope
- Ege – name of a village (ON *eiki*=oak grove)
- Eide – isthmus (ON *eið*=isthmus)
- Engen – name of several farms (from ON *eng*=meadow)
- Finstad – Finn's farmstead (ON *staðr*=farmstead, dwelling)
- Føyen – named after a small island now known as Føynland in Vestfold county (*fé*=cattle + *øy*=island)
- Gill – ravine
- Hagen – pasture (ON *hagi*=enclosure, pasture); also a farm name

- Haugen – hill, mound; also a farm name
- Holm – islet (ON *holmr*)
- Holt – forest
- Ihle – well, spring (from *ila*)
- Island – icy land (from *is*=ice + *land*=land)
- Jahr – edge
- Kjellberg – from ON *kelda*=spring, source of water + *berg*=mountain
- Kjos – valley
- Landvik – land inlet, a Norwegian town (*land*=land + *vik*=inlet)
- Langeland/Langland – lang=long + land=land, farmstead
- Lykken – name of a farmstead (from *lykkja*=enclosure)
- Melby – modern form of Meðalbýr=middle farm (from ON *meðal*=middle + *býr*=farm)
- Mørk – name of several farmsteads (from ON *mork*=wood)
- Myklebust – large farm (from ON *mikill*=large + *bólsaðr*=farm)
- Nordhal/Nordal – a place name in Sunnmøre (from ON *norðr*=north + *dalr*=dale, valley)
- Nygård – new farm (*ny*=new + *gård*=farm, yard)
- Ødegård – deserted farm (*øde*=deserted, empty + *gård* =farm, yard)
- Østby – name of farmsteads (from ON *aust*=east + *býr*=farm, village)
- Rosholt – from either of two farms named Røsholt (from ON *ruð*=clearing + *holt*=grove, wood)
- Sandvik – sandy bay (*sand*=sand + *vik*=bay, inlet)
- Seehuus – house by the sea (*see*=sea + *huus*=house)
- Stokholm – protruding piece of land (*skyta*=to shoot + *holme*=islet)
- Ulberg – mountain wolf (*ulfr*=wolf + *berg*=mountain)
- Ure – rocky slope meadows
- Værnes – name of village, originally Vannes (*var*=calm, quiet + *nes*=headland)
- Vig/Vik – from ON *vík*=bay, inlet)

By comparison to this huge variety of habitational names, the list of occupational surnames is rather scant. They are not usually found as surnames, but rather as place names (Fiske – from *fiskr*=fish + *vin*=meadow; Smedstad=smith's place). Here is a short list.

- Fiske – fisherman, fish seller
- Hammersmed – blacksmith (*hammer*=hammer; *smed*= smith)
- Horn – horn carver or horn player
- Kusken – driver
- Møller – miller
- Snekkeren – carpenter

SWEDISH

Like the rest of the Nordic countries, Sweden used the patronymic naming system. This practice was abolished in Sweden with theNames Adoption Act of 1901, when everyone was obligated to adopt a permanent surname. At that time, most Swedes who had not already taken a hereditary name chose to 'freeze' their primary patronyms, making them hereditary secondary patronyms. They form the most common group of surnames in Sweden today.

Hereditary names began appearing in Sweden around the 15th and 16th centuries almost exclusively within the aristocracy. Many consisted of heraldic symbols of the family coat of arms. At first these were added to the patronymic as an identifier to form the family name, but after circa 1600, noble families started using these names without the patronymic. Some typical surnames of the **nobility** were (Ahrholdt, 2004-2022a):

- Anckarsvärd – *anckar/ankar*=anchor + *svärd*=sword
- Cederström – *ceder*=cedar + *ström*=stream
- Cronhielm – cron/kron=crown + *hielm/hjälm*=helm
- Gyllenhammar – *gyllen*=golden + *hammar*=hammer
- Gyllenhielm – *gyllen*=golden + *hielm/hjälm*=helm
- Gyllenstierna – *gyllen*=golden + *stjärna*=star
- Oxenstierna – *oxen*= oxen + *stjärna*=star
- Stålhandske – *stål*=steel + *handske*=glove
- Ulfsparre – *sparre*=chevron – heraldry

A much smaller number of surnames are **humanist** names, whose use spread from Germany and Central Europe around the 16th century to Sweden and the rest of Scandinavia. They consist of a partial name plus a Greek or Latin ending, such as ***-aeus, -ander, -ius, -sis, -us, -aeus.*** These names were popular among the clergy, as well as scholars, scientists and other academics, who also Latinized or Grecicized their given names.

- Anders Eriksson → Andreas Erici
- Erik Henriksson → Ericus Stephani
- Olof Johansson → Olaeus Johannis
- Lars Karlsson → Laurentius Caroli
- Karl Pettersson → Carolus Petri

By the beginning of the 17th century, young clerics started creating family names by translating into Latin the names of their birth places, be they farms, villages, or parishes. This custom gave birth to names like: Celsius (from Högen, meaning 'the mound', translated to Celsus), Cavallius (from Håldala, meaning 'hollow valley', translated to *cava vallis*), Montanus (from Berg). Some chose to Latinize the name of their place of origin by adding *ius* to it, yielding new surnames such as: Abelius, Bergius, Darelius, Lothigius, Netzelius and Nobelius. Generations later, many of their descendants would shorten these surnames to Abel, Darrell, or Nobel.

A common suffix that remains to the present day was ***-ander***, derived from the Greek word *andró*, meaning 'man'. It was usually added to the first syllable of a toponymic. It gave rise to surnames like Ahlander, Bellander, Erlander, Gullander, Levander, Olander, Svalander and Ysander, and many more (Olsson, 1981).

In the 17th century, soldiers who joined the army and the navy had to give up their patronymic surnames and adopt **military** names. The soldiers in each company had to have unique names which were assigned to them by their superiors. When they left the military, the soldiers took back their patronymic names and their military names could be transferred to new recruits. Later on, in the 19th century, many soldiers kept their military name, which often became hereditary.

In the army, many military names referred to personal characteristics or objects related to battle.

- Hurtig – bold
- Lång – tall
- Modig – courageous
- Munter – cheerful
- Rolig – funny
- Sabel – saber
- Skarpsvärd – sharp sword
- Sköld – shield

- Stark – strong
- Stolt – proud
- Strid – battle
- Tapper – brave

The navy names were associated with nautical terms or words related to the sea.

- Abborre – perch, the fish
- Ankare – anchor
- Block – pulley
- Hake – hook
- Lax – salmon
- Mast – mast
- Segel – sail
- Storm – gale
- Strand – shore
- Vind – wind

In the 17th and 18th centuries, the middle classes, particularly artisans and town dwellers, followed the nobility in choosing hereditary names. Many were ornamental names, which consisted of creative combinations of elements from nature, sometimes with the suffix *-man*, the name of the family farm or town of origin, or an occupation.

Tradesmen and craftsmen were often given occupational nicknames, such as *Hans bagare* (Hans the baker), *Sven smed* (Sven the smith), or *Johann skräddare* (John the tailor). As people began to adopt heritable surnames, these occupations did not necessarily describe their descendants, so most of these surnames did not survive to the present day.

Typical Swedish **ornamental** names are (Ahrholdt, 2004-2022b):

- Berglund – *berg*=mountain + *lund*=grove
- Bergman – *berg*=mountain + *man*=man
- Bergqvist – *berg*=mountain + *qvist*=twig
- Bergström – *berg*=mountain + *ström*=stream
- Eklund – *ek*=oak + *lund*=grove
- Engström – *en*=juniper + *ström*=stream
- Forsberg – *fors*=rapids + *berg*=mountain
- Holmberg – *holme*=island + *berg*=mountain
- Lindberg – *lind*=linden + *berg*=mountain
- Lindgren – *lind*=linden + *gren*=branch

- Lindqvist – *lind*=linden + *qvist*=twig
- Lindström – *lind*=linden + *ström*=stream
- Löfgren – *löv/löf*=leaf + *gren*=branch
- Lundberg – *lund*=grove + *berg*=mountain
- Lundgren – *lund*=grove + *gren*=branch
- Lundqvist – *lund*=grove + *qvist*=twig
- Nyström – *ny*=new + *ström*=stream
- Sandberg – *sand*=sand + *berg*=mountain
- Sjöberg – *sjö*=lake + *berg*=mountain
- Wikström – *vik/wik*=bay + *ström*=stream

The majority of Swedes today have patronymic surnames, the 'frozen' patronymic names of their ancestors, formed by adding *-son* to a male's—or occasionally, a female's—genitive form of a given name, hence the double 's'.

Of the 20 most common Swedish surnames compiled in December 2020, 19 are patronymic (Kamann, 2021).

1. **Andersson** (son of Anders)
2. **Johansson** (son of Johan)
3. **Karlsson** (son of Karl)
4. **Nilsson** (son of Nils)
5. **Eriksson** (son of Erik)
6. **Larsson** (son of Lars)
7. **Olsson** (son of Olle)
8. **Persson** (son of Per)
9. **Svensson** (son of Sven)
10. **Gustafsson** (son of Gustav)
11. **Pettersson** (son of Petter)
12. **Jonsson** (son of Jon)
13. **Jansson** (son of Jan)
14. **Hansson** (son of Hans)
15. **Bengtsson** (son of Bengt)
16. **Jönsson** (son of Jön)
17. **Lindberg** (linden – mountain)
18. **Jakobsson** (son of Jakob)
19. **Magnusson** (son of Magnus)
20. **Olofsson** (son of Olof)

Since there were a relatively small number of traditional male given names, these names have been recycled from generation to generation until they became permanent and hereditary. Not surprisingly, there is only one patronymic surname among the next 10 most common ones. The rest are ornamental, topographic surnames.

21. **Lindström** (linden – stream)
22. **Lindqvist** (linden – twig)
23. **Lindgren** (linden – branch)
24. **Berg** (mountain)
25. **Axelsson** (son of Axel)
26. **Bergström** (mountain – stream)
27. **Lundberg** (grove – mountain)
28. **Lind** (linden)
29. **Lundgren** (grove – branch)
30. **Lundgvist** (grove – twig)

FINNISH

Finnish surnames are as interesting as they are diverse. To better understand their development, it is important to know some historical facts. Finland was an independent country until about the 13th century, when it was conquered by Sweden during the Crusades. Finnish remained the language of the peasantry, while the church and the nobility used Swedish primarily. Finland remained part of the Kingdom of Sweden and the realm of the Catholic Church until 1809, when most of its territory was ceded to the Russian Empire at the end of the Finnish War. Finland finally became an independent country in 1917, after the Russian Bolshevik revolution. Yet, it was the Finnish language from before the 13th century that formed the basis for surname formation.

Finnish surnames follow three main naming traditions: one for western Finland, one for eastern Finland, and one for the nobility, the clergy, the military and the bourgeoisie. Before the 20th century, Finland was mostly an agrarian society, so many of the names of western Finns consisted of the name of the area, farm, or homestead they inhabited followed by the locative suffix ***-la*** or ***-lä***. A farm name often bore the name of the male owner or was descriptive of its location. This name could change when people moved from one farm to another.

Eastern Finns, on the other hand, had an agricultural system that required them to move often from one cultivable area to another (Stief, 2019), which brought about a need for permanent family names. Families started adopting surnames as early as the 13th century, and by the 16th century, they became hereditary. These names were formed by adding the suffix ***-nen,*** historically a diminutive, first to patronyms, then to topographic names. One could think of the suffix *-la* as referring to a place and *-nen* to the people living there. In the 19th century, when eastern Sweden became part of Russia, these surnames extended to the rest of the country and *-nen* became the most common suffix in Finnish surnames to the present day.

Around the 16th century, members of the nobility and middle classes with some education began to choose Swedish surnames rather than Finnish ones because they were considered prestigious. The clergy chose humanist names derived from Latin, which often ended in ***-ius.***

Starting at the end of the 17th century, soldiers were assigned temporary surnames unrelated to their family names that they held throughout their military service. These names could be descriptive or based on the name of their barracks, in which case this name was shared with all the soldiers in that barracks.

In the 19th century, tradesmen and craftsmen in urban areas began to adopt permanent surnames. These were often occupational names translated from Finnish to Swedish or vice-versa, or they were ornamental Swedish names.

The most common type of surname in Finland had been patronymic, based on the father's given name. These were more popular in western Finland, where the Swedish influence was prevalent. However, patronymic surnames were used in official documents only until the end of the 19th century. Unlike in the rest of the Nordic countries, Finnish patronymics were not transferred into permanent surnames, and since they were no longer required by law, they gradually fell out of use.

After Finns became independent in 1917 and were no longer under Swedish rule, they began to feel pride in their Finnish heritage. During this time, many who had Swedish names or who had previously changed their Finnish names to Swedish ones took or took back their Finnish surnames. So today it isn't always easy to know with certainty whether a surname originated in the east or the west.

By far the largest group of Finnish surnames are **topographic** or **habitational**, describing a geographic feature of an area inhabited by ancestors.

- Aho, Ahonen – forest clearing
- Aalto, Aaltonen – wave
- Halla – fallow field, frost
- Haapala – aspen
- Harmaajärvi – gray lake
- Heitala – sand
- Huhta – glade, clearing
- Järvi, Järvela, Järvinen – lake
- Jokela, Jokinen – of the river
- Kallio – rock
- Keto – meadow, grassy field
- Kivi, Kivela – stone
- Koivisto – birch tree (*koivu* + *-sto*)
- Koskinen – rapids (*koski*)
- Laakso, Laaksonen – valley
- Lahti, Lahtinen – bay, cove
- Laine – ocean wave
- Lehto, Lehtonen – small grove or forest
- Luoma – creek, small river
- Mäkelä, Mäkinen – hill (*mäki*)
- Niemi, Nieminen – peninsula, cape
- Nurmi – field, pasture
- Oja – dike, ditch
- Peltonen – field (*pelto*)
- Ranta, Rantanen – beach, shore
- Rinnie – slope, hillside (*rinne*)
- Ruoho – grass
- Saari, Saarinen – island
- Salminen – strait (*salmi*)
- Salo, Salonen – forest

Another group of surnames are derived from **personal names**, most of which have the suffix ***-la.***

- Annala –from personal name *Anna* + suffix *-la*
- Erkkila – farm name from personal name *Erkki* + suffix *-la*
- Eskola – farm name from personal name *Esko* + suffix *-la*

- Heikki, Heikkilä, Heikkinen – from personal name *Heikki* (diminutive of *Henrik)*
- Jutila – from personal name *Juti, Jutti* (diminutive of *Johannes*) + suffix *-la*
- Kylonen – from personal name *Kyllia, Kylloi, Kylio* + suffix *-nen*
- Laitinen – from personal name *Laiti* + suffix *-nen*
- Lassila – from Swedish personal name *Lasse, Lassi* + locational suffix *-la*
- Martikainen – from personal name *Martti* + suffix *-nen*
- Nikula – from personal name *Nikku* + suffix *-la* (diminutive of *Nicholas*)
- Pekkanen – from personal name *Pekka* + suffix *-nen*
- Pietila – from personal name *Pieti* (diminutive of *Peter*) + suffix *-la*
- Tuomala – from personal name *Tuomas* (variation of *Thomas*) + suffix *-la*

Descriptive surnames

- Keranen – with a round head or cropped haircut
- Korhonen – deaf (*korho*)
- Kurtti – courteous
- Leino – weak, sad
- Mustonen – black (*musta*)
- Partanen – bearded
- Pulska – fat
- Vanhanen – old

Occupational surnames

- Kangas – garment maker or merchant
- Karjala – cattle herdsman
- Kemppainen – soldier, warrior
- Korpi – basket maker or vendor
- Rautio – smith
- Seppä, Seppäla, Seppänen – blacksmith
- Suutari – shoemaker

Surnames derived from the flora and fauna of a region belong to individuals who lived or worked at farmsteads in those areas and their descendants.

Surnames derived from **plants**

- Honkala – pine tree
- Karerva – heather
- Koivisto – birch tree
- Kuusisto – spruce
- Lehtinen – leaf
- Leppanen – alder tree

Surnames derived from **animals**

- Karhu – bear
- Karppinen – carp (from *karppi*, Germanic origin)
- Kokko – eagle (from *kotka*)
- Orava – squirrel
- Peura – deer, reindeer
- Punkki – mite
- Sikanen – little pigs
- Susi – wolf

Geographic surnames

- Hämäläinen – from the *Häme* province in central Finland
- Karjalainen – from *Karjala* (*Karelia*), an area on the border of Finland and Russia

Ethnic surnames

- Saksa – Saxon (from Germanic *Sachs*)
- Ruotsalainen – Swede
- Venäläinen – Russian

The most common surnames in Finland as of February 2022 are (Statista, 2022b):

1. **Korhonen** (deaf, but also referring to an aloof, clumsy, or silly person)
2. **Virtanen** (one who dwells near a river)
3. **Mäkinen** (one who lives in a hilly area)
4. **Nieminen** (one who lives on or near a small peninsula)
5. **Mäkelä** (one who dwells in a hilly area)
6. **Hämäläinen** (from the *Häme* district in the southwest of Finland)
7. **Laine** (one who lives near the coast)
8. **Heikkinen** (offspring of Heikki, lord of the manor)

9. **Koskinen** (one who dwells near the rapids)
10. **Järvinen** (one who lives near a lake)
11. **Lehtonen** (one who lives near a grove or orchard)
12. **Lehtinen** (ornamental name from *lehti*=leaf)
13. **Saarinen** (one who lives on an island)
14. **Salminen** (one who dwells near a strait)
15. **Heinonen** (a descendant of *Heino* or someone who lived in his household)
16. **Heikkilä** (someone from a farmstead headed by someone named *Heikki*)
17. **Niemi** (one from a farm on a peninsula)
18. **Kinnunen** (uncertain origin, possibly derivative of Swedish *skinn*=animal skin)
19. **Salonen** (ornamental name from *Salo*; late adoption in 19-20th centuries)
20. **Turunen** (name of uncertain meaning)

Finland's first Family Name Act, issued in 1920, made permanent family names mandatory and gave everyone one year to acquire one. From 1930 until 1985, married women were obligated by law to adopt their husband's surname. The Family Name Act of 1985 allowed both spouses to choose to either keep their birth surnames, hyphenate them or for either spouse to adopt the other's (Wallius, 2019). Some even chose to create a brand new surname for their new life together. Although the number of spouses keeping their surnames after marriage has been increasing steadily since 1986, the majority of women today still either take their husband's surname or hyphenate their two surnames upon marriage. Hyphenating two surnames can sometimes yield some very amusing combinations, such as Pulska-Orava (fat squirrel), Nälkäinen-Karhu (hungry bear), or Susi-Sikanen (wolf-little pigs).

The more recent Name Act of 2017 further liberalized surname options by allowing couples complete freedom of name choice for them and their children.

THE BALTIC STATES

Estonia, Latvia and Lithuania are considered Baltic states because of their geographic location on the shores of the Baltic Sea. Of the three, the Estonian language is not Baltic, but is close to Finnish; it belongs to the Finno-Ugric branch of the Uralic language family rather than the Indo-European language group.

ESTONIAN

Compared to the rest of Europe, Estonians were late in adopting surnames, not including, of course, Icelanders, who have never adopted the custom of inheritable fixed family names. The few Estonians who had surnames at the beginning of the 19th century were mainly members of the nobility and the clergy.

Before the introduction of surnames, Estonians were identified by the name of the manor or farm with which they were associated, followed by a patronymic and a first name, or for short, the farm name and the given name. For instance, Karroma Hans was Hans, master of Karroma farm (Lestal, 2014).

After the emancipation of serfs in 1816-1819, Estonian peasants who had been liberated from serfdom were given surnames in the 1820s in the central and southern province of Livland (Livonia) and in the 1830s in the northern province of Estland (Esthonia). This process was conducted by the Baltic German landowners, who tended to be partial to German names.

At the end of World War I, with the independence of Estonia after the disintegration of the Russian Empire, the movement to Estonianize surnames, particularly German ones, began in earnest in the 1920s, culminating in the 1930s with hundreds of thousands of Estonians adopting Estonian family names en masse. This phenomenon was similar to the neighboring Finns' efforts to adapt their surnames from Swedish to Finnish, and to such movements in other parts of Eastern and Northern Europe (Raun, 2012).

The most common surnames are Estonian, with Russian in second place. Estonians have at least one given name, often two, and rarely three, and one surname typically inherited from the father, although a child could be given the mother's name. Women usually take their husband's name upon marriage; some keep their own and others hyphenate both surnames. Less common options are for the husband to take the wife's surname or for both to have hyphenated names.

The majority of Estonian surnames are derived from nature—topographic features, plants or animals. Others designate an occupation. We should keep in mind that many of these names were chosen during the forced Estonianization of the population.

Topographic surnames are derived from forms and features of land surfaces. This is the largest group of surnames since many root words can be combined in multiple ways to form compound nouns.

- Äär – border, boundary
- Aas – open grassy area
- Allik – water source
- Hiis – grove
- Jäälaid – ice islet
- Jäämets – ice forest
- Jääväli – ice field
- Järv – lake
- Jõgi – river
- Kalda, Kallas – shore
- Kalju – cliff
- Kaljulaid – cliff islet
- Kaljumäe – cliff hill
- Kaljupank – cliff bank
- Kivi, Kivik, Kivikas, Kiviste – stone
- Kosk – waterfall
- Laine – wave
- Läte – fountain, wellspring
- Lättemäe – spring mountain (*lätte*=spring/fountain + *mäe*=hill/mountain)
- Liiv – sand
- Mägi – mountain
- Mändla – pine area
- Mändmäe – pine hill
- Mändmets – pine forest
- Mändoja – pine stream
- Mändsoo – pine swamp
- Meri – sea
- Mets – forest
- Oja – brook
- Oru – valley (*org*)
- Rand – beach
- Saar – island
- Soosar – swamp island

Surnames derived from **plants**

- Haab – aspen
- Hernes – pea
- Jalakas – elm
- Jõhvik, Jõhvikas – cranberry
- Kadak – juniper
- Kask, Kaasik – birch
- Kirsipuu – cherry tree
- Kirss – cherry
- Kõrvits – pumpkin
- Kuslapuu – honeysuckle tree
- Laur – laurel
- Leht – leaf
- Lill, Lille – flower
- Lillakas – lilac
- Mänd – pine
- Nõges – nettle
- Õun – apple
- Paju – willow
- Pärn – linden
- Remmel, Remmelgas – willow
- Rõigas – radish
- Saar – ash
- Sirel – lilac
- Tamm – oak
- Tõru – acorn
- Uba – bean
- Vaarik – raspberry

Surnames derived from **animals**

- Aul – long-tailed duck
- Hani – goose
- Haug – pike
- Hirv – deer
- Hunt – wolf
- Ilves – lynx
- Jänes – hare
- Kägu, Käo – cuckoo
- Kala – fish

- Kana – hen, chicken
- Karu – bear
- Kass, Kõuts – cat
- Kits, Kruup – goat
- Konn – frog
- Kotkas – eagle
- Krabi – crab
- Kukk, Kikkas – rooster (*kikas*)
- Kull – hawk
- Kurg – stork
- Lammas – sheep
- Lehmus – cow (*lehm*)
- Lõoke – lark
- Luik – swan
- Nirk – stoat
- Ööbik – nightingale
- Orav – squirrel
- Parts – duck (*part*)
- Ploom – plum
- Rebane – fox
- Ronk – raven
- Sikk, Sikkel – billy goat
- Varblane, Värbu – sparrow (*värb*)
- Vares – crow
- Vint – finch

Surnames derived from **occupations**

- Jääger – hunter
- Juske – peddler (*harjusk*)
- Kalamees – fisherman
- Kangur – weaver
- Kaupmees – shopkeeper
- Kingsepp – shoemaker
- Kokk – cook
- Kübarsepp – hat maker (*kübar*=hat + *sepp*=smith)
- Kuningas – king
- Kütt – hunter
- Leivat, Leivategija – bread maker, baker
- Madrus – sailor

- Mölder – miller
- Nahkur – tanner
- Putsep – cooper
- Ratsep – tailor
- Raudsepp – blacksmith
- Ruutli – knights
- Sepp – smith

A smaller group of names are derived from **descriptive** words.

- Aus – honest
- Hea – good
- Helliste – affectionate
- Hepp – lively
- Ilus – beautiful
- Kallis – beloved
- Kaunis – beautiful
- Kirt – wrinkled
- Kõverjalg – bow-legged
- Lemba, Lember, Lempu – loving, affectionate (*lembe*)
- Liik – kind
- Pent – funny, eccentric (*pentsik*)
- Ränk – heavy, burdensome, wicked
- Tark – wise
- Truu – faithful
- Varrak – rich

The 10 most common Estonian surnames in 2022 seem to have been adopted during the process of Estonianization in the 1920s and '30s. They also represent a majority among the top 20 names, with only one (Ivanov) Russian surname (Surnam, 2022a).

1. **Tamm** (oak)
2. **Saar** (ash)
3. **Sepp** (smith)
4. **Kask** (birch)
5. **Mägi** (mountain)
6. **Kukk** (rooster)
7. **Rebane** (fox)
8. **Koppel** (paddock, pasture)
9. **Karu** (bear)

10. **Ilves** (lynch)
11. **Lepik** (alder wood)
12. **Oja** (brook)
13. **Ivanov** (Russian patronymic meaning 'son of Ivan')
14. **Kuusk** (spruce)
15. **Kaasik** (birch)
16. **Cuca** (uncertain meaning in Estonian)
17. **Luik** (swan)
18. **Raudsepp** (blacksmith)
19. **Vaher** (maple)
20. **Kallas** (shore)

LATVIAN

The oldest Latvian surnames were held by noblemen, free merchants and craftsmen living in towns, and they mostly originated from German names, due to German being an official language in Latvia at that time. After the end of serfdom in the early 19th century, the emancipated serfs were able to choose their surnames. Many chose ethnic Latvian names, most commonly derived from nature and often in diminutive forms. They constitute the largest single group of surnames in Latvia today. However, a considerable number opted for Germanic surnames in the hope that they might improve their social standing (LSM, 2020). A much smaller group of names were of Finnic (Livonian or Estonian) origin.

After Latvia became part of Imperial Russia in late 19th century, Latvian names became Russified, following the three-name patterns of Russian names. This continued into the 20th century with the emergence of the Soviet Union. However, the surname endings had to reflect Latvian surname patterns, as did the surnames of all residents of Latvia, no matter their origin.

There are normally different surname endings for men and women. Male family names, as well as given names, typically end in ***-s***, ***-š*** or ***-is***, and female names tend to end in ***-a*** or ***-e***, with some exceptions for foreign names.

- Bērziņš (M)/Bērziņa (F) – birch (diminutive in the masculine)

- Gulbis (M)/Gulbe (F) – swan
- Kalniņš (M)/Kalniņa (F) – mountain, hill (diminutive in the masculine)

The Latvianization of Russian names, as well as of the Polish and Belarussian surnames of some residents of the southeastern province of Latgale, which bordered Belarus, consisted of changing the final *-ski/-cki* to *-skis/-ckis*, *-czyk* to ***-čiks*** or *-vich/-wicz* to ***-vičs***, such as *Sokolovski / Sokolovska, Baldunčiks / Baldunčika* or *Ratkevičs / Ratkeviča*.

Most Latvian surnames are derived from the homestead of one's ancestors and from the topographic features of the land and its flora and fauna. The surnames in the following categories are given in the masculine form.

Topographic surnames

- Avotiņš – spring, water source
- Celmiņš – tree stump (*celms*)
- Dārziņš – garden
- Ezeriņš – lake (*ezers*)
- Grīva – creek (one form)
- Kalniņš – mountain, hill (*kalns*)
- Krastiņš – coast (*krasts*)
- Krūmiņš – bush, shrub (*krūms*)
- Līcis – bay
- Salinš – inhabitant of an island (*sala*=island)
- Upitis – river (*upe*)

Surnames derived from names of **plants**

- Āboliņš – clover
- Ābols, Ābele – apple, apple tree
- Alksnis – alder tree
- Apsītis – aspen tree (*apse*)
- Auziņš – oats (*auzas*)
- Bērziņš – birch tree (*bērzs*)
- Eglītis – spruce tree (*egle*)
- Kaņeps – hemp
- Kārkliņš – osier (*kārkls*)
- Kļaviņš – maple (*kļava*)
- Liepiņš – linden tree (*liepa)*
- Osis – ash tree

- Ozols, Ozoliņš – oak tree
- Paeglis – juniper
- Plūme – plum, plum tree
- Priedītis – pine tree (*priede*)
- Rudzītis – rye
- Vīksna – elm
- Vītols, Vītoliņš – willow
- Zirnis – pea

Surnames derived from names of **animals**

- Balodis – pigeon
- Briedis – deer
- Cālītis – chick (*cālis*)
- Caunis – marten (*caune*)
- Cīrulis – lark
- Dzenis – woodpecker
- Gailis, Gailītis – rooster (*gailis*)
- Gulbis – swan
- Lācis – bear (*lāce*)
- Lūsis – lynx
- Strazds – blackbird
- Vanags – hawk
- Vilks, Vilciņš – wolf
- Zaķis – hare, rabbit
- Zvirbulis – sparrow

Some surnames are derived from **occupations**

- Adītājs – knitter
- Arājs – ploughman
- Kalējs – blacksmith
- Kučieris – coachman
- Kurpnieks – shoemaker
- Mērnieks – surveyor
- Mucenieks – cooper
- Mūrnieks – mason
- Podnieks – potter
- Puķe – flower seller (*puķe*=flower)
- Ratnieks – wheelwright
- Vecvagars – old overseer (*vecs*=old + *vagars*=overseer)

- Zvejnieks – fisherman

A smaller group comprises **descriptive** surnames based on personal appearance or personality traits.

- Baltiņš – white
- Čaklais – diligent
- Garš – tall
- Gudrs – wise
- Jumārs – round (from Livonian *jumeršķi*)
- Kreilis – left-handed
- Kurls – deaf
- Lazdiņš – hazel (*lazda*)
- Punduris – dwarf
- Ruds – red-haired
- Sirmais – grey-haired

A few names denote **nationality**.

- Krievs, Krieviņš – Russian
- Leitis – Lithuanian
- Pinnis – Finn
- Polis – Pole
- Turks – Turk
- Vācietis – German
- Zviedrs – Swede

The list of the 20 most common surnames in Latvia in 2022 includes masculine (M) and feminine (F) versions (Surnam, 2022b).

1. **Berzina** (birch – F)
2. **Ozola** (oak – F)
3. **Ivanova** (Russian patronymic – F)
4. **Kalnina** (mountain, hill – F)
5. **Ozolina** (oak – F, diminutive)
6. **Berziņš** (birch – M)
7. **Ozols** (oak – M)
8. **Jansone** (Scandinavian patronymic – F)
9. **Ivanovs** (Russian patronymic – M)
10. **Kalniņš** (mountain, hill – M)
11. **Ozoliņš** (oak – M, diminutive)
12. **Liepina** (linden tree – F)

13. **Eglite** (spruce – F)
14. **Arpa** (uncertain origin, possibly Turkish – F)
15. **Balode** (pigeon – F)
16. **Krūmina** (bush – F)
17. **Andersone** (Scandinavian patronymic – F)
18. **Vasiljieva** (Russian patronymic – F)
19. **Dreimanis** (Latvian of uncertain meaning – M)
20. **Jansons** (Scandinavian patronymic – M)

It is important to note that the strict rules governing Latvian names extend to foreign-born Latvian nationals and to those (usually women) who assumed their foreign spouse's family name. They are also reflected in how Latvians refer to foreigners by name. Instead of maintaining the original spelling and trying to approximate as closely as possible the actual pronunciation, they change the spelling to conform to the highly phonetic Latvian orthography. So, they might say and write *Donalds Tramps* (Donald Trump), *Hoakins Finikss* (Joaquin Phoenix), or *Žerārs Depardjē* (Gerard Depardieu) (Mawhood, 2016).

The same fate would befall immigrants and visitors to Latvia for an extended stay. This has given rise to numerous lawsuits, but the plaintiffs have usually lost their case.

LITHUANIAN

Lithuanian and Latvian belong to the Baltic branch of the Indo-European language family. Both Lithuanian and Latvian surnames have different endings for men and women. Lithuanian also differentiates between married and single women. One could think of these endings as titles that have been suffixed to the name root, which would result in different surnames for a mother, father and daughter in the same family.

Table 5 summarizes the distribution of surname suffixes as a function of gender and marital status. Masculine surnames typically end in ***-as***, ***-is***, or ***-(i)us***. Unmarried women's surnames end in ***-aitė***, ***-ytė***, ***-ūtė*** or ***-tė***. Married women's surnames traditionally consisted of their husband's name plus the suffix ***-ienė***, but this tradition has gradually been changing (Kudirka, 1991). Women may keep their birth surname after they marry and/or they may choose the marriage-neutral suffix -è. Sons inherit their father's surname unchanged. However, there is a tradition in smaller villages to address unmarried sons by their father's surname plus the diminutive suffix ***-(i)ukas***, i.e. Adamkiukas, Jankauskiukas.

Table 5. Lithuanian surname suffixes by gender and marital status

Surname suffixes for all men	**Surname suffixes for single women**	**Surname suffixes for married women**	**Surname suffixes for all women**
Adamk**us**	Adamk**utė**	Adamk**ienė**	Adamk**ė**
Jankausk**as**	Jankausk**aitė**	Jankausk**ienė**	Jankausk**ė**
Kazlausk**as**	Kazlausk**aitė**	Kazlausk**ienė**	Kazlausk**ė**
Stankevič**ius**	Stankevič**iūtė**	Stankevič**ienė**	Stankevič**ė**

Lithuanian surnames were first adopted in the 15th century by members of the nobility and gradually spread to the towns by the end of the 17th century, and finally to the peasantry by the end of the 18th century. Most of these names were of foreign origin, such as Greek, Latin, Hebrew, Slavic and Germanic. A great number of them are derived from Greek given names and were brought to Lithuania via the Slavic and Germanic countries through Christianity.

Many surnames are patronymics derived from male personal names, which themselves are Lithuanized versions of Greek, Slavic, Germanic, Latin or Hebrew given names.

Patronymics or derivations from **personal names**

- Adamkevicius, Adamkus, Adomas – patronymic from the personal name *Adomas* (Hebrew *Adam*=man)
- Andris, Andromaitis – patronymic from a variant of the given name *Andrys* (Greek *Andreas*=manly, courageous)
- Bernotas – patronymic from a variant of the personal name *Bernardas*
- Butkus – diminutive of *Budkintas*; derivative from personal name *Budzisław* (Polish for 'awakening glory')
- Danis, Danielis – derivative from personal name *Daniel* (Hebrew for 'God is my judge')

- Gabrys – derivative from the personal name *Gabrieliu* (Hebrew for 'God is my strength')
- Jankauskas – patronymic form of personal name *Janek* (from Polish *Jan*)
- Janulis – patronymic from *Janul* (Polish nickname for *Jan*)
- Jonaitis – from personal name *Jonas* (Hebrew *Yonah*=dove)
- Juska – from a nickname of the personal name *Justus*
- Kubilus – derivative from personal name *Jakub/Jokubas* (Hebrew for 'supplanting')
- Markūnas – patronymic from the personal name *Markus*
- Petraitis, Petruškevičius – from the given name *Petras* (from Latin *Petrus*=rock)
- Petrauskas – patronymic form of the given name *Petras*
- Šimkus – patronymic from nickname *Szimkoor* (Polish) or *Shimko* (Belorussian)
- Šimonis – patronymic from *Šimas/Simonas* (from Hebrew *Shim'on*=he has heard)
- Urbonas – from personal name *Urbanus* (Latin *Urbānus*=city dweller)
- Vasiliauskas – from personal name *Vasil* (from Greek *Basileus*=royal, kingly, a reference to Christ, king of the heavens)
- Vidas – diminutive form of personal name *Vidmantas* (*vyd*=to see + *mantus*=intelligent)
- Vitkus – diminutive form of personal name *Výtautas* (*vyti*=to guide + *tauta*=people)

Occupational surnames

- Backus – barrel maker
- Bakshis – fighter or boxer
- Bernius – German-Latinized form of *Berner*, a Lithuanian derivative of *bérnas*=farmhand
- Degutis – someone who made or sold tar (*degutas*=tar)
- Kalvis, Kalvelis, Kalvaitis – blacksmith
- Kavaliauskas – blacksmith (from Polish *Kowalski; kowal*=blacksmith)
- Meizys – barley or wheat farmer
- Molis – brick maker (*clay*)
- Pisula – informal nickname for *scribe* or *clerk* (from Polish *pisać*=to write*)*

- Sakalauskas – falconer (derived from the given name *Sokol*= falcon in several Slavic languages)
- Šaulis – rifleman (*šaulys*)

Descriptive surnames

- Balčiūnas – patronymic from given name *Balčius* (from Lithuanian *baltas*=white)
- Balkus – nickname for a person with white hair or very light complexion (from Polish *biały*=white)
- Balthis, Baltis – descriptive nickname (from *baltas*=white)
- Bayus – rich (from Russian *bai*)
- Dobis – from Duoba (Polish *Doba*) a shortened form of Slavic personal name describing a brave person (*dob*=courageous, noble)
- Kairys, Kairelis – left-handed (*kairė*=left side)
- Kanas – miser
- Klukas – foolish (*klukius*)
- Mazeika – small, short (*mazas*)
- Melis – blue
- Moris – lazy (*morys*)
- Žilinskas – equivalent of Polish surname *Zieliński* (from Polish *zieleń*=green)

Surnames derived from **animal names**

- Gagas – gander (possibly also an occupational name for a keeper of geese)
- Gaida – rooster (*gaidys*)
- Kazlauskas – equivalent of Polish surname Kozłowski (from Polish *kozioł*=male goat, also possibly a toponymic for several Polish cities, such as *Kozłow* or *Kozłowo*)
- Vilkas – wolf
- Zukas – white rabbit (reduced form of *Žukauskas*)
- Žukauskas – from Polish *żuk* (beetle)

Topographic surnames

- Galinis – someone who lived at the end of a road or village (*galas*=end)
- Laukaitis – a person who lives in or near a field (*laukas*=field)
- Miskinis – someone who lived in or near a forest (*miškinis*=forest, forest spirit)
- Užugiris – someone who lives across the forest (*už girios*)

Geographic/toponymic surnames

- Bardzilauskas – Lithuanian version of *Bordzilovskiy* (Belarussian from the village of *Bordzily*)
- Kaunas – originally from the Lithuanian city of the same name
- Kazlauskas – equivalent of Polish surname *Kozlowski*, given to someone from any of several Polish cities, such as *Kozłow* or *Kozłowo*, originally from Polish *kozioł*=male goat
- Perske, Persky – from the village of *Pershai* in Belarus, or possibly *Perki* in Lithuania
- Smolenskas – Lithuanian form of *Smolensky*, toponymic of *Smolensk*, a region in Western Russia
- Valanĉiūnas – from the place name *Valanĉiūnai*
- Višneviškas – from the Belarussian town of *Višneva* that was originally Lithuanian, called *Višnevas*
- Vitkauskas – equivalent of Polish surname Witkowski, given to someone from Witkowo, Witków, or Witkowice
- Žemaitis, Žemaitaitis – lowlander, from a region in western Lithuania (*Žemaitéjè*)

Ethnic surnames

- Gudaitis – Belorussian (gudas)

The list of the 20 most common surnames in Lithuania includes masculine (M) and feminine (F) versions (Forebears, 2012-2022f).

1. **Jankauskienė** (from Polish *Jankowski*, from personal name *Janek* – F)
2. **Kazlauskienė** (from Polish *Kozłowski; kozioł*=billy goat – F)
3. **Petrauskas** (from personal name *Petras*; from Latin *Petrus*=rock – M)
4. **Petrauskienė** (from personal name *Petras*; from Latin *Petrus*=rock – F)
5. **Stankevičienė** (from Polish *Stanisławski,* from personal name *Stanisław* – F)
6. **Jankauskas** (from Polish *Jankowski*, from personal name *Janek* – M)
7. **Kazlauskas** (from Polish *Kozłowski; kozioł*=billy goat – M)
8. **Stankevičius** (from Polish *Stanisławski,* from personal name *Stanisław* – M)

9. **Paulauskienė** ((from personal name *Paulius/Paulinius*, Latin for *small* – F)
10. **Vasiliauskienė** (from Greek personal name *Vasil*=royal, kingly – F)
11. **Vasiliauskas** (from Greek personal name *Vasil*=royal, kingly – M)
12. **Butkus** (from Polish personal name *Budzisław*=awakening glory – M)
13. **Balčiūnienė** (from personal name *Balcius*, from Lithuanian *baltas*=white – F)
14. **Žukauskienė** (from Polish *Żukowski*, from *żuk*=beetle – F)
15. **Urbonienė** (from personal name *Urbanus*, Latin for *city dweller* – F)
16. **Kavaliauskienė** (from Polish *Kowalski; kowal*=blacksmith – F)
17. **Navickienė** (from Polish Nowicki
18. **Urbonas** (from personal name *Urbanus*, Latin for *city dweller* – M)
19. **Ramanauskienė** (from Polish *Romanowski*, from personal name *Roman* – F)
20. **Stankevič** (from Polish *Stanisławski,* from personal name *Stanisław* – M)

The Slavic Countries

Slavic countries are generally categorized along geographic lines into three major subgoups:

- Eastern Slavic – Russian, Ukrainian, Belarusian
- Western Slavic – Polish, Czech, Slovak
- Southern Slavic – Slovenian/Slovene, Serbian, Croatian, Bosnian, Macedonian, Bulgarian

Slavic (Slavonic) surnames appeared at different times in different areas. As in most European countries, they appeared in the late Middle Ages in more densely populated areas as a way to differentiate among people with the same given name living in close proximity. In some rural areas, however, they were not used until as recently as the early 20th century. They reflect patronymic descent, occupations, geographic origin, personal characteristics or they are derived from natural objects, like animals and plants. Surnames are hereditary and generally passed patrilineally from father to children. Many Slavic surnames have masculine and feminine versions. The most common surnames are patronymic.

Eastern Slavic

Eastern Slavic—Russian, Ukrainian, Belarusian—people use a tripartite naming system: the given name, the patronymic and the surname. The patronymic is the middle name and it's derived from the father's first name plus a suffix, which differs by gender. Patronymics are used in combination with the full first name in forms of address as a sign of respect. The third element in the name is the surname or family name, which usually also uses different suffixes for males and females. All legal and identity documents must contain all three names.

When women marry, they retain their given name and patronymic, but normally adopt their husband's last name. In this case, one would not be able to distinguish a maiden surname from a married surname because the suffixes are the same, having to rely on the patronymic middle name to help with further identification.

Eastern Slavic languages have grammatical cases and genders, which are also applied to names. Not all surnames change with gender, however. If the surname is an adjective, gender agreement is made. If it's a noun, it is not. Most Russian names are inflected according to gender, whereas Ukrainian and Belarusian surnames rarely are.

RUSSIAN

Every Russian person's name is made up of three elements: the given name, the patronymic middle name, and the surname. It is very common for first names to have a variety of nicknames, some more intuitive than others. They are used in informal situations among close friends and family members to indicate familiarity and affection. As a form of address, the use of the first name followed by the patronymic indicates respect. The patronymic is derived from the father's first name plus the suffix *-ovich* or *-evich* (son of) or *-ovna* or *-evna* (daughter of).

The most common surname endings, usually indicative of patronymic surnames, are: ***-ov/-ova, -ev/-eva*** or ***-in/-ina,*** for masculine/feminine, respectively. The endings ***-sky/skaya*** can sometimes be of Polish or Belarusian origin. The following are examples of full Russian names. The patronymic middle name endings are underlined.

- Leonid Nikolaievich **Andreyev**
- Olga Nikolaievna **Andreyeva**
- Vladimir Ivanovich **Petrov**
- Maria Ivanovna **Petrova**
- Igor Borisovich **Volkonsky**

The feminine surname endings for 'daughter of' and 'wife of' are the same. The differences are clear in the patronymic second name.

Occupational surnames

- Bocharov/Bocharova – barrel (*bochar*) maker
- Bortsov/Bortsova – wrestler (*borets*)
- Chugunov/Chugunova – cast iron (*chugun*) worker
- Kuznetsov/Kuznetsova – blacksmith (*kuznets*)
- Pastukhov/Pastukhova – shepherd (*pastukh*)
- Popov/Popova – priest (*pop*)
- Portnov/Portnova – tailor (*portnoi*)

Descriptive surnames

- Gorbachev/Gorbacheva – hunchback (*gorbun*)
- Nosov/Nosova – big nose (*nos*)
- Sedov/Sedova – gray-haired (*sedoi*)
- Smirnov/Smirnova – quiet, still (*smirnoy*)
- Tolstov/Tolstova, Tolstoy/Tolstaya – stout, fat (*tolsty*)

Geographic surnames

- Belsky/Belskaya – from Bielsk
- Gurin/Gurina – from Gurin, Belarus
- Moskvin/Moskvina – from Moskva (Moscow
- Riazanov/Riazanova – from Riazan
- Smolensky/Smolenskaia – from Smolensk

Surnames derived from **animal** names

- Golubev/Golubeva – dove, pigeon (*golub*)
- Gusev/Guseva – goose (*gus*)
- Komarov/Komarova – mosquito (*komar*)
- Kozlov/Kozlova – goat (*kozel*)
- Lebedev/Levedeva – swan (*lebed*)
- Orlov/Orlova – eagle (*orel*)
- Sokolov/Sokolova – falcon, hawk (*sokol*)
- Solovyov/Solovyova – nightingale (*solovey*)
- Volkov/Volkova – wolf (*volk*)
- Zaitsev/Zaitseva – hare (*zayats*)

The 10 most common Russian surnames are (Alexey, 2013-2019):

1. **Ivanov / Ivanova** (descendant of Ivan)
2. **Smirnov / Smirnova** (peaceful, calm, gentle)
3. **Kuznetsov / Kuznetsova** (blacksmith)
4. **Popov / Popova** (priest)
5. **Vasiliev / Vasilieva** (descendant of Vasily)
6. **Petrov / Petrova** (descendant of Pyotr)
7. **Sokolov / Sokolova** (falcon, hawk)
8. **Mikhailov / Mikhailova** (descendant of Mikhail)
9. **Fedorov / Fedorova** (descendant of Fedor/Feodor)
10. **Morozov / Morozova** (possibly a nickname, from the Russian word *moroz*=frost)

UKRAINIAN

The Ukrainian tripartite naming system is very similar to the Russian one, with some minor differences in the suffixes. The patronymic (middle name) endings are: *-ovych* (son of) and *-ivna/ -evna* (daughter of). Some common surname endings are:

-enko (Yushchenko, Tymoshenko) – distinctively Ukrainian, mostly patronymic or occupational, but can be found in all the categories

-chuk, -chak, -uk, -iuk (Kravchuk, Romaniuk, Maksymchak) – usually patronymic

-vich/-vych (Domitrovich, Pavlovich, Popovich) – patronymic

-ko (Boiko, Pavlichko) – diminutive ending with patronymic meaning

-yshyn/-ishyn (Kostyshyn, Voloshyn)

-sky/-ska (Olesky, Krushelnytska) – habitational; changes according to gender

-ov/-ova, -ev/-eva (Azarov/Azarova, Zaytsev/Zaytseva) – changes according to gender

Many of these suffixes are shared by Russian, Ukrainian and Belorusian surnames. That is not the case with names ending in ***-enko***, which are not only the most common, but also the most readily recognizable Ukrainian surnames. As Slavutych (1962) points out, they are not found among any other Slavic group. When *-enko* surnames are found in other places, they are sure to indicate Ukrainian descent.

Most Ukrainian surnames do not change according to gender except those that are adjectives: ***-sky/-ska, -ov/-ova, -ev/-eva, -in/-ina, -iy, -oy, -yy/-aya.*** Here are some examples of full names:

- Viktor Andriyovych **Yushchenko**
- Yulia Volodymyivna **Tymoshenko**
- Leonid Makarovych **Kravchuk**
- Olga Vasilyevna **Kondratyuk**
- Oleg Sergeyevych **Zhitkov**
- Oksana Sergeyevna **Zhitkova**

The following lists represent male surnames in the most common categories.

Patronymic surnames, the largest group of Ukranian surnames, are formed from a male ancestor's given name or a diminutive form of it. Since Slavic diminutives are numerous and widely used, there can be a variety of patronymic surnames that come from one given name. For instance, possible surnames based on the name Ivan include: Ivaniv, Ivankiv, Ivasiv, Ivashko, Ivashenko, Ivashchenko, Ivanenko, Ivaniuk.

Occupational surnames

- Bondar (Bondarenko, Bondaruk) – barrel maker, cooper
- Bortnik – beekeeper
- Chumak – salt trader
- Datsyuk – service provider
- Honchar (Honcharenko, Honcharuk) – potter, ceramist
- Hudzik – button maker
- Kalashnik – Kalaches (a sort of bread) maker
- Kolesnik (Kolisnychenko) – wheelwright
- Koval – blacksmith
- Kozar – goat herder
- Kravets (Kravchenko, Kravchuk) – tailor
- Kushnir (Kushnirenko, Kushniruk) – furrier
- Oliinyk – vegetable oil manufacturer
- Pachenko – fisher
- Ponomarenko (Ponomarchuk) – clergyman
- Portnoy – tailor
- Reznikov – ritual slaughterer
- Rybalka – fisherman (from *ryba*=fish)
- Shevchenko – cobbler (*shvets*)
- Skliar – glazier

Descriptive surnames

- Buchko – noisy person (from *bucha*=noise)
- Chernenko – black, dark (from *chorny*= black)
- Horbanenko – hunchback
- Hudzik – small man (from *hudzik*=button)
- Kryvonis – curved nose
- Lisko – bald man (from *lysyj*=bald male) or fox, cunning person (from *lis*=fox, cunning)

Geographic (habitational) surnames – most endings are variations of ***-ski (-sky, -skiy)***

- Boiko – resident of Western Ukraine
- Kalzuny – person who lives in a muddy area
- Krasinski – person from areas of Ukraine or Belarus, such as Krasnaya, Krasna, Krasnoe
- Lipka – someone who lives near a lime tree (from *lipa*=lime tree)
- Lubarsky – people from the Lyubar region in Volhynia, Ukraine, or from Lubarka, Lithuania
- Malinski – someone from Malin in Ukraine
- Olensky – someone from the region of Olewsk in Ukraine
- Zelinski – a person from Zelenki in Ukraine
- Zolochivskiy – from Zolochiv in Ukraine

Surnames derived from **animal** names

- Baran – ram
- Buhaj – bull
- Chornovil – black ox
- Gogol – common goldeneye (type of duck)
- Kotyk, Koshka – cat
- Kovbe – type of fish
- Medved – bear
- Shpak – starling
- Soroka – magpie
- Vorona – crow
- Vovk – wolf
- Zaysev – hare

Surnames derived from **plants**

- Bereza – birch
- Kalyna – cranberry
- Kapusta – cabbage
- Kulbaba – dandelion

The 10 most common surnames in Ukraine are (Forebears, 2012-2022g):

1. **Melnyk** (occupational – miller)
2. **Shevchenko** (occupational – cobbler, from *shvets*)
3. **Bondarenko** (occupational – cooper, barrel maker)

4. **Kovalenko** (form of Koval, occupational – blacksmith)
5. **Boiko** (habitational – resident of Western Ukraine)
6. **Tkachenko** (occupational – weaver, from *tkach*)
7. **Kravchecko** (occupational – tailor, from *kravets*)
8. **Kovalchuk** (form of Koval, occupational – blacksmith)
9. **Koval** (occupational – blacksmith)
10. **Shevchuk** (occupational – cobbler, from *shvets*)

Belarusian

Just as we've seen with Ukrainian surnames, Belarusian surnames tend to be nouns, therefore they are not inflected for gender. The endings ***-ski/-skaya*** are used as adjectives, therefore they do change according to gender, as do ***-ov/-ova, -ev/-eva.*** There are many surnames that are common in both Ukraine and Belarus.

There are also surnames that are nouns without any suffixes. They are much more common in Ukrainian and Belarusian names than in Russian names. Many of these are derived from animal names.

Patronymic (middle name) endings

-avich/-avna for names ending in consonants
-(y)evich/-(y)evna for names ending in vowels

Surname endings

-vich (-vič), -ich (-ič): Karpovich, Stankevich, Komich, Kuznich, Savich

-ski/-skaya: Vasilevski, Vasilevskaya, Malinovsky, Kozlovskaya (marked for gender)

-ka, -enka: Lukašenka, Jakavienka

-ko, -enko: Boyko, Makarenko, Vasilenko, Prokopenko

-ak, -onak, -yonak: Rusak, Burak, Manionak

-uk, -yuk, -chuk (čuk): Kravchuk, Romanyuk, Pinchuk, Savchuk, Masiuk

-ienia: Majsienia, Hierasimienia, Jurčenia

-ov/-ova, -ev/-eva: Azarov/Azarova, Zaytsev/Zaytseva (marked for gender)

Here are some examples of full Belarusian names:

- Aleksandr Antonavich **Chizhevsky**
- Olga Antonavna **Chizhevskaya**
- Svetlana Stanislavavna **Klimuk**
- Dárya Ignatyevna **Dómracheva**
- Mikhail Ignatyevič **Dómrachev**

When it comes to Eastern Slavic names, we must remember that they are written in the Cyrillic alphabet; therefore, the transliteration into Latin script is often done without a uniform standard, or rather, with a standard specific to each republic. This accounts for variations among certain letter clusters, such as: ***-ski/-sky/-skiy, -vich/-vič,*** -enko/ienko/-jenko/-yenko, etc.

Patronymic surnames (***-vich/vič***)

- Alexievich – son of Alexey
- Antonovich – son of Anton
- Ivanova – daughter of Ivan
- Petrovich – son of Piotr
- Pyatkevich – fifth-born child
- Žydovič – of Jewish descent

Occupational surnames

- Drapkin – coachman (from *drabki*= light cart)
- Portnoy – tailor (*portnoj*)
- Žaŭniarovič – soldier (*žaŭnier*)

Descriptive surnames

- Durko – foolish, dumb (*durny*)
- Harbachoŭ – hunchback (Belarusian equivalent of Gorbachev)
- Kisly – sour, acidic
- Lyskin – bald, hairless (*lysy*)
- Novikaŭ – new to town

Habitational surnames (***-ski/-sky***)

- Gavazansky – from the town of Gavezhnov
- Kovaleski – from a place called Kovali
- Slucki – from Sluck, a town in the Minsk region
- Tolinski – from the town of Stólin

Derived from **animal names**

- Arlianionak – eagle (*arol*)
- Chaykov – seagull (*chayka*)
- Filin – owl
- Koška – cat
- Kot – tomcat
- Krysin – rat (*krysa*)
- Salaŭjoŭ – nightingale (*salaviej*)
- Zhaba – toad, frog
- Zyk – beetle

Surnames derived from **given names**

- Abramčuk – from Abram
- Jančanka – from Jan
- Prokopenko/Prakapienka – from Prokopiy
- Yakubovich – from Yakub

Surnames derived from **nicknames**

- Abramienia – from diminutive form of Abram
- Adamčyk – from diminutive form of Adam
- Ivashkin – from the diminutive Ivashka, from Ivan
- Janačkin – from a diminutive form of Jan

The 10 most common Belarusian surnames are (WorldNames, 2020):

1. **Ivanov** (son of Ivan)
2. **Ivanova** (daughter of Ivan)
3. **Novik** (newcomer – M)
4. **Zhuk** (beetle)
5. **Moroz** (frost)
6. **Novikova** (newcomer – F)
7. **Kotova** (cat, fem.)
8. **Petrov** (son of Piotr)
9. **Novikov** (descendant of newcomer – M)
10. **Volkova** (wolf – F)

WESTERN SLAVIC

Western Slavic people include Czechs, Slovaks and Poles. Their names consist of a given name and a surname, which usually reflects the gender of its owner. The Czech and Slovak languages are very closely related and are mutually intelligible, which is reflected in the surnames. Due to geographic proximity and a shared history, which gave way to ethnic mixing over centuries, one can see the effect of German names on Czech surnames, especially in the feminine form (Schmidtová/Šmitová, Müllerová/Mullerová), and to a greater extent of Hungarian on Slovak surnames. Unlike Eastern Slavic surnames, which are inflected for gender only if they're adjectives, Czech and Slovak add -***ova*** to the masculine form of surnames regardless of whether they are nouns or adjectives.

CZECH

Czech surnames may be descriptive, occupational, they may be derived from a given name, an animal, a plant, a geographical location, or even a verb. This last one is an interesting and unusual group of surnames formed from a present tense, a past participle or an imperative form of a verb. The following is a list of masculine surnames in these categories.

Descriptive of a personal characteristic of an ancestor

- Babinec – coward
- Bilek, Bilko – fair-haired person, from *bílý* (white)
- Hluchý – deaf
- Kulhanek – someone who walks with a limp
- Malý – small
- Sis – sweet, from German *süss*
- Škudlárek – stingy person
- Veselý – cheerful

Occupational surnames

- Fristenky – beet farmer
- Hladik – furniture polisher
- Hudek – fiddler
- Koči – coachman, driver
- Kolář – wheeler

- Kovář – blacksmith
- Krajca – tailor
- Kuchař – cook, chef
- Sedlák – landowner
- Sklenář – glassworker
- Švec – shoemaker

Surnames derived from **a given name**

- Adamek – from Adam
- Duchek – from Duchoslav
- Eliáš – from Elias
- Marek – from Mark
- Mašek – from Matěj, Matúš and Mattiáš (Matthew)

Surnames derived from **animals**

- Beruška – ladybug
- Čáp – stork
- Holub, Holoubek – pigeon
- Jelínek – little deer
- Ježek – hedgehog
- Kocourek – little tomcat
- Liška – fox
- Sokol – falcon
- Sýkora/ Sejkora – titmouse
- Vlk – wolf
- Vrabec – sparrow

Surnames derived from **plants**

- Cibulka – little onion
- Fialka – violet
- Hruška – pear
- Jahoda – strawberry
- Javůrek – young maple
- Konvalinka – lily of the valley
- Malina – raspberry
- Růžička – little rose
- Vrba – willow

Geographical surnames

- Moravec – Moravian

- Němec – German
- Nepomucký – from Nepomuk
- Rosický – from Rosice u Brna
- Slezák – Silesian
- Slovensky – from Slovakia

Surnames **indicative of an action**

- Hrabal – he raked
- Musil – he had to
- Navratil – he returned
- Pospíšil – he hurried
- Skočdopole – Jump in a field!
- Zdražil – he raised the price

The 10 most common Czech surnames (M/F) are (Lednicka, 2014):

1. **Novák / Nováková** (someone new to town)
2. **Svoboda / Svobodová** (free man, subordinate only to the king)
3. **Novotný / Novotná** (someone new, similar to Novák)
4. **Dvořak / Dvořaková** (free man who owned a farm, from *dvůr*= farm)
5. **Černy / Černá** (person with dark skin or hair, from *černy*= black)
6. **Procházka / Procházková** (someone who traveled some distance, itinerant)
7. **Kučera / Kučerová** (someone with curly hair)
8. **Veselý / Veselá** (a happy, good-natured person)
9. **Horák / Horáková** (someone who comes from the hills or mountains, a highlander)
10. **Krejči** (occupational name for tailor; it does not change according to gender)

SLOVAK

Similarly to the Czechs, Slovaks do not usually have a patronymic middle name and their surnames distinguish gender by adding the suffix *-ová* in most cases to a form of the masculine surname. However, the recent tendency toward equality in naming in many European countries can also be seen in Slovakia, where more and more women are opting to not add the *-ová* ending. Still, changing long-standing traditions takes time, sometimes several generations.

The 10 most common surnames (M/F) in Slovakia are (Jano, 2022):

1. **Horváth / Horváthová** (Hungarian name for Croat)
2. **Kováč / Kováčová** (occupational name for makers of metal tools and weapons)
3. **Varga / Vargová** (occupational name for *cobbler* – Hungarian origin)
4. **Tóth / Tóthová** (Hungarian name for Slav from Hungary)
5. **Nagy / Nagyová** (descriptive name – Hungarian for *big*)
6. **Baláž / Balážová** (Slovak derivation of male name Blažek; also a Hungarian name)
7. **Szabó / Szabová** (occupational name – Hungarian for *tailor*)
8. **Molnár / Molnárová** (occupational name – Hungarian for *miller*)
9. **Balog / Balogová** (toponymic word for a settlement in Eastern Slovakia)
10. **Lukáč / Lukáčova** (Slovak derivation of male name Lukáš, a Slovak name)

It may seem odd that almost all of the most common surnames in Slovakia are actually Hungarian, but not so odd if we think of its history. Slovakia was part of the Austria-Hungary Kingdom for many centuries, and for much of that time Hungarian was the official language.

The largest group of Slovak surnames are occupational. Others are descriptive of physical or personality traits (often derived from nicknames), geographical, or they may be derived from names of saints, from the Old or New Testament, and from things in nature. The following is a list of masculine surnames in these categories.

Occupational surnames

- Bača – shepherd
- Fristensky – beet farmer
- Gajdoš – bagpipe player
- Holič – barber
- Hudák – fiddler
- Kocis – coahman
- Kollár – wheelwright
- Kováč, Kováčik – smith
- Kuchár – cook
- Lokaj – footman (servant)
- Maliar – painter
- Mäsiar – butcher
- Mazáč – bricklayer
- Mlynár, Molnár – miller
- Pekár – baker
- Puškár – rifle maker
- Robotnik – laborer
- Szabó – tailor
- Varga – cobbler
- Zeleznik – iron man

Descriptive surnames

- Biely – white- or light-haired person
- Čierny – black, dark
- Dlhý, Dlhoš – long
- Krásný – beautiful
- Malý – small
- Ópatrný – cautious
- Plačko – crying man
- Ryšavý – red-haired
- Št'astný – happy
- Tichý – silent
- Tupý – blunt, dull
- Veselý – joyous
- Zelená – green

Geographical surnames

- Balog – from the settlement Balog nad Ipl'om in Eastern Slovakia

- Horváth – Hungarian name for Croat
- Németh – Hungarian name for German
- Novák, Novotný – newcomer to an area
- Polák – from Poland
- Rusnák – from Russia
- Tóth – Hungarian name for Slavic people

Surnames derived from **first names**

- Ďuriška – from Juraj (George)
- Jančo, Janoška – from Ján (John)
- Lukáč – from Lukáš (Luke)
- Matuška – from Matúš (Matthew)
- Michalko – from Michal (Michael)
- Petráš, Peterka, Petrík – from Peter
- Štefanec – from Štefan (Stephen)

Surnames derived from **nature** (plants, animals, foods)

- Chren – horseradish
- Chrobák – beetle
- Cibuľka – little onion
- Dolina – valley
- Holub – pigeon
- Kocur – tom cat
- Komár – mosquito
- Koreň – root
- Malina – raspberry
- Medvedík – little bear
- Mráz – frost
- Polievka – soup
- Repa – beet
- Slanina – bacon

POLISH

Until about the 12th century CE, people had only one name. To eliminate confusion between people with the same given name, they were described as the son of someone or, when that was not enough, the brother of someone was added. People were also identified by their occupation and, when necessary, by the father's name and occupation, by place of birth or residence, by a descriptive nickname, or by a combination of any of them.

By the 14th century it was commonplace to identify people by using two words, at first among members of the upper classes, then among peasants and in official documents. It wasn't until the end of the 17th century that second names became inherited, again beginning with the nobility, and slowly spreading to all social classes.

Polish surnames fall into three major categories: geographic (toponymic and topographic), cognominal, and patronymic (and rarely matronymic).

Toponymic and **topographic** surnames form the oldest and most numerous group, as they comprise more than a third of the one thousand most common Polish surnames. Originally claimed by members of the nobility who were landowners, these names were derived from the names of their estates, followed by the suffix ***-ski*** or one of its alternate forms (-***cki, -zki, -dzki***). At the time, these surnames were highly prestigious, but with the passage of time, they were adopted by the middle and lower classes of society to indicate the geographic origin of the family. Names ending in ***-ski*** or any of its variants have a corresponding feminine form, -***ska***. Polish used to have special feminine suffixes. A woman who had never married used her father's surname with the suffix ***-owna*** or ***-anka***. A married woman or a widow used her husband's surname with the suffix -***owa*** or ***-ina/-yna***. Although this custom is still being used in certain remote areas, it has become outdated. The tendency is toward a uniform surname for both men and women. The following are a few examples of toponymic surnames, with the corresponding feminine forms, where applicable.

- Górski / Górska (mountain) – from a snowy, mountainous area
- Jankowski / Jankowska – from the town Jankowo or Jankow
- Kaminski / Kaminska (stone) – from any of several villages named *Kamien*

- Kozlowski / Kozlowska – from any of several towns named Kozlow or Kozlowo
- Krakowski / Krakowska – from Krakow
- Mazur, Mazurski / Mazurska – from Masuria
- Rusnak – from Russia
- Sadowski / Sadowska – garden, orchard
- Warszawski / Warsawska – from Warsaw

Eventually, these names began to lose the exclusive toponymic or possessive meaning as they were used widely in a neutral sense. The *-ski* suffix was added to existing surnames, especially to cognominal ones (see below), and soon became the most common and most easily recognizable ending of Polish surnames.

Cognominal surnames were derived from nicknames, which were usually based on occupations or physical or personality traits. Some occupational and many descriptive surnames end in ***-ek***, a common nickname suffix. Many occupational names took on the suffix ***-ski*** (feminine *-ska*) and sometimes others (***-czyk, -ik, -ek, -ewski***).

Occupational surnames

- Cieślak – carpenter
- Kaczmarek → Kaczmarski – innkeeper
- Kowal → Kowalski, Kowalczyk, Kowalik, Kowalewski – blacksmith
- Krawiek – tailor
- Marszalek → Marszalski – a marshall, a high ranking military or government official
- Mencher – miller, flour dealer
- Ryba → Rybiński – fisherman, fish seller
- Slusar → Slusarski – locksmith
- Sobol → Sobolski– fur trader
- Starosta – foreman, leader
- Szewczyk – shoemaker
- Zdun → Zdunowski (also toponymic, from the town of Zduny) – potter

Descriptive surnames

- Klimek – merciful
- Kosmatka – shaggy, hairy
- Nosek – small nose

- Novak, Nowakow, Nowakowski, Nowacki, and Nowicki – new
- Paszek, Pawlak, Maly – small, little
- Starek – old
- Wysocki – tall

Patronymic surnames are derived from a given name of a father or ancestor and can have any of a wide variety of endings, of which ***-wicz*** is by far the most common.

-wicz, -owicz, -ewicz

- Antoniewicz – offspring of Antoni
- Piotrowicz – offspring od Piotr (Peter)
- Rabinowicz – offspring of the rabbi
- Szymonowicz/Szymonowic – offspring of Szymon (Simon)

-yk, -czyz, -ak, szczak, -czak

- Adamczyk – offspring of Adam
- Filipczyk – offspring of Filip
- Łukaszewski – offspring of Łukasz (Luke)
- Staszczyk, Stachowiak, Stasiak – offspring of Stanislaw

Surnames derived from **first names** (as patronyms or toponyms)

- Adamczewski, Adamczyk, Adamowski, Adamski – derived from Adam or Adamowo / Adamczewo (towns)
- Jan, Jachowicz, Janicki, Jankowski, Janowski – derived from Jan (John) or Janowo / Jankowo / Janice (towns)
- Łukasinski, Łukaszewski, Łukaszewicz – derived from Łukasz (Luke) or Łukasin (town)
- Marek – from Mark
- Stanisławczak, Stanisławiak, Stanisławek and Stanisławski – from Stanislaw

Surnames derived from **animals**

- Kaczka – duck
- Koziel – male goat
- Lis – fox (possibly of someone who was thought to be sly or crafty)
- Myszka, Mysz – mouse
- Sikora, Sikorka – titmouse
- Sokolowski – falcon
- Sowka – owl
- Wrona – crow
- Zuraw – crane

The 10 most common surnames in Poland in January 2020 as reported by the Polish Ministry of Digital Affairs (Czarnecka, 2020) are:

1. **Nowak** (from *nowy*, new)
2. **Kowalski / Kowalska** (from *kowal*, blacksmith)
3. **Wiśniewski / Wiśniewska** (from wiśnia, cherry)
4. **Wójcik** (from *wójt*, chief officer of a group of villages)
5. **Kowalczyk** (from *kowal*, blacksmith)
6. **Kamiński / Kamińska** (from *kamień*, stone)
7. **Lewandowski/ Lewandowska** (from *Lewandów*, town name from 'lavender tree')
8. **Zieliński / Zielińska** (from *zielony*, green)
9. **Szymański / Szymańska** (from *Szymon*, equivalent to Simon)
10. **Woźniak** (from *woźny*, civil servant)

Southern Slavic

The Southern Slavs today include Bulgarians and the residents of the lands of former Yugoslavia (literally South Slavia)—Slovenia, Croatia, Bosnia and Herzegovina, Montenegro, Serbia, and North Macedonia. After the breakup of Yugoslavia in the early 1990s, these republics became independent nations. When analyzing surnames, Serbian and Croatian names are examined together because of their close similarity. The other territorial surnames are described separately, as there are patterns specific to each of them.

Southern Slavs usually have one given name and one surname, which is passed on patrilineally and is not marked for gender. There has recently been a tendency for people to keep their birth names after marriage, occasionally to hyphenate them, and even give their children last names from both parents. This tendency is not specific to Slavic countries, but reflects a universal trend toward equity in society.

The South Slavic standard languages are Serbo-Croatian (Serbian, Croatian, Bosnian, Montenegrin) and Slovene in the west, and Bulgarian and Macedonian in the east. The western group of Southern Slavs show very similar surname patterns. Their names are mostly patronymic (and some matronymic, mainly in Serbia and Croatia), occupational, descriptive, or they may be derivations from names of plants or animals.

The following symbols will be used for brevity to designate these ethno-linguistic groups:

- S: Serbian
- C: Croatian
- Sv: Slovene
- B: Bosnian

SLOVENIAN/SLOVENE

Aside from some of the surname patterns Slovenians share with other Southern Slavs, there are several types of surnames that are specific to them (Borovnik, 2020). Slovenian surnames typically end in:

-ič (patronymic, equivalent to Serbo-Croatian ***-ić***, this is the most common Slovenian surname suffix), e.g., Božič, Marusič, Janežič, Martinčič, Adamič

-nik (mostly Slovenian, possibly indicative of a toponymic surname), e.g., Robnik, Kolnik, Plečnik, Brezovnik

-ar (Slovenian, Serbian, Croatian, often indicative of an occupational surname), e.g., Brezar, Kolar, Mlinar, Bučar, Pečar

-ec (typical for Slovenian, Czech and Slovak surnames), e.g., Korošec, Godec, Pevec, Kranjec (or the alternate forms Kranjc or Krajnc)

-šek (although uncommon, this suffix is used exclusively in Slovenian surnames), e.g., Drnovšek, Gorenšek, Dolinšek, Bezenšek

The following lists represent the most common categories of Slovenian surnames:

Patronymic/Matronymic surnames

- Gregorič – offspring of Gregor
- Ivanc – offspring of Ivan
- Jankovič – offspring of Janko
- Marusič – offspring of Marija
- Zupančič – offspring of a community leader

Occupational surnames

- Godec – musician
- Kmet – farmer
- Kopač– digger
- Kopitar – farrier, horse shoer (*kopito*=hoof)
- Košir – basket maker (*koš*=basket)
- Kuhar – cook
- Pevec – singer
- Podriznik – priestly vestiment, possibly a maker of such clothes
- Ribič – fisherman
- Šuštar – shoemaker
- Zagar – sawyer
- Žavbi – ointment maker (žavba=ointment, cream)
- Žitnik – baker, rye dealer (*žito*=rye)
- Zupan – community leader, mayor (*župan*)

Descriptive surnames

- Pleško – bald (*pleša*=bald patch)
- Razbornik – prudent (*razborit*)

Habitational / Toponymic surnames

- Halozan – from the Halože region of Slovenia
- Kotnik – from a remote area (*kot*=corner)
- Krajnc – someone from the region of Carniola (*Kranjska*)
- Potočnik – someone who lives near a stream, brook (*potok*)
- Pušnik – someone living near uncultivated land (*pušča*)
- Vrhovnik – someone from the mountain top (*vrh*=peak, summit)

Surnames derived from **first names**

- Gregorčič – from Gregor

- Ivanek, Ivanič, Ivanuša, Ivanušič – from Ivan (John)
- Majdič – from Majda (Slovenian and Arabic feminine name meaning 'noble glory')
- Pavlič – from Pavel (Paul)
- Petrič – from Peter
- Tomažič – from Tomaž (Thomas)
- Uršič – from Urša (Ursula)

Surnames derived from **animal names** – descriptive of physical or mental characteristics

- Bolha – flea
- Jazbec – badger
- Jelen – deer
- Jež – hedgehog
- Kos – blackbird
- Maček – male cat
- Sraka – magpie
- Zajc – hare
- Zec – rabbit, also (SCB)
- Žižek – black bug
- Zver – beast

According to the Republic of Slovenia Statistical Office (2021), the 10 most common surnames in Slovenia are:

1. **Novak** – name for someone who is new to a village
2. **Horvat** – demonym for Croatian
3. **Kovačič** – son of a blacksmith
4. **Krajnc** – toponym for someone from the region of Carniola (*Kranjska*)
5. **Zupančič** – descendant of a mayor (*župan*)
6. **Kovač** – blacksmith
7. **Potočnik** – someone who lived near a brook (*potok*)
8. **Mlakar** – someone who lived near water (*mlaka*, meaning pool, puddle)
9. **Vidmar** – someone who lived on land belonging to the church
10. **Kos** – blackbird

Serbian and Croatian

Patronymic and **matronymic** surnamesThere are several patronymic and matronymic suffixes, of which ***-ić*** is the most common, making up about two thirds of all Serbian surnames, as well as a majority of Croatian surnames. It is often transcribed as *-ich* or *-itch*. The suffix ***-ić*** is a masculine diminutive suffix, which can be combined with either the name or the occupation of a parent to create a patronymic or a matronymic surname. Other such suffixes are: ***-ov, -ev, -in***, and the less common ***-ski*** (and its variants ***-cki/čki/ški***), which are the Slavic possessive suffix; thus Nikola's son becomes Nikolin, Petar's son Petrov, and Jovan's son Jovanov. The two suffixes are often combined, most commonly as ***-ović***. Some common Serbian and Croatian patronymic surnames are:

- Adamić (C) – offspring of Adam
- Andrejević (S) – offspring of Andrej
- Andrejić (SC) – offspring of Andrej
- Bogdanović (SC) – offspring of Bogdan
- Bogdanić (C) – offspring of Bogdan
- Branković (SC) – offspring of Branko
- Dragović (SC) – offspring of Drago
- Filipović (SC) – offspring of Filip
- Ivancović (SC) – offspring of Ivan
- Janković (SC) – offspring of Janko
- Pavlović (SC) – offspring of Pavle
- Popović (SC) – offspring of a priest
- Todorić (SC), Todorović (S), Todorovac (B) – offspring of Todor
- Vasilijević (S) – offspring of Vasilije

Although less common, matronymic surnames are widespread among Serbs and Croats. When surnames were first standardized in Serbia in 1851, they were to be based on the name of the eldest living relative in the household, who, in some cases, were women. Here are some examples:

- Anđelić (SC) – offspring of Anđela
- Anić (C) – offspring of Ana
- Babić (SCSv) – offspring of *baba* (old woman)
- Janjić (SC) – offspring of Janja
- Katić (SC) – offspring of Katja
- Klarić(CSv) – offspring of Klara

- Marić (S), Marušić (C), Marusič (Sv) – offspring of Marija
- Milenić (SC) – offspring of Milena
- Miličić (SC) – offspring of Milica
- Natalić (SC) – offspring of Natalia
- Zorić (C) – offspring of Zora

Occupational surnames

- Čoban (SC) – shepherd (cognate of Turkish *Çoban*)
- Klobučar (C) – hatmaker
- Košar (C) – basket maker or seller, from *koš* (basket)
- Kovač (SCSvB) – blacksmith
- Kravar(C) – cow herder
- Krčmar (C) – innkeeper
- Krznar (C) – furrier, Krznarić (C) – offspring of furrier,
- Kujundžić (SC) – silversmith
- Lončar (SCSvB) – potter
- Mesarić (C), Mesaroš (S) – from *mesar* (butcher)
- Mornar – sailor, Mornarić (C) – offspring of sailor
- Stolar (C) – carpenter
- Tkalčić (C) – weaver
- Travar (SC) – herbalist
- Vitez (SC) – knight, Vitezić – offspring of knight
- Zlatar (SC) – goldsmith, jeweler

Descriptive surnames

- Ćosić (SC) – beardless (*ćosav)*
- Crnčević (SC) – black (*crn*)
- Divjak (SC) – savage
- Glasnović (C) – loud
- Gluhak (C) – deaf
- Grbić (SCSv) – hunchback (*grba*=hump)
- Mladić (SC) – young (*mlad/a*)
- Novak (SC) – newcomer
- Šarinić (C) – colorful

Surnames derived from **nature**

- Gavran (SC) – raven
- Golub, Golubić, Golubovec (C), Golob (Sv) – pigeon
- Jablanović (C) – from *jablan* (poplar)
- Janjić (SC) – from *janje* (lamb)
- Kokotović (SC) – from *kokot* (rooster)
- Lipnjak (C) – from *lipa* (linden tree)
- Mažuranić (C) – from mažuran (marjoram)
- Pevec (C) – rooster
- Rak (Sl), Rakić (S), Rakinac (C) – from *rak* (crab, lobster)
- Rodić (SC) – stork
- Ružić (SC) – from *ruža* (rose)
- Vuk (SC), Vucan (S), Volk/Vovk (Sv) – wolf
- Žabek (C) – from *žaba* (frog)
- Zajc (Sv) – from *zajec* (hare)
- Zek (SCSvB) – rabbit

The 10 most common surnames in Serbia are (Kursar, 2022):

1. **Jovanović** – offspring of Jovan (John)
2. **Petrović** – offspring of Petar (Peter)
3. **Nikolić** – offspring of Nikola (Nicholas)
4. **Marković** – offspring of Marko (Mark)
5. **Đorđević** – offspring of Đorđe (George)
6. **Stojanović** – offspring of Stojan (Stoyan)
7. **Ilić** – offspring of Ilija (Elijah)
8. **Stanković** – offspring of Stanko (Stanislav)
9. **Pavlović** – offspring of Pavle (Paul)
10. **Milošević** – offspring of Miloš (Miles)

The 10 most common surnames in Croatia are (CroatiaWeek, 2020):

1. **Knežević** – descendant of a prince (*kniz*)
2. **Horvat** – demonym for Croatian
3. **Kovačević** (variant of Kovačić) – offspring of a blacksmith (patronymic and occupational)
4. **Pavlović** – offspring of Pavel
5. **Blažević** – derived from Blaž
6. **Božić** – offspring of Božo
7. **Lovrić** – offspring of Lovro

8. **Babić** – offspring of an old woman
9. **Marković** – offspring of Marko
10. **Bošnjak** – demonym for Bosnian

BOSNIAN

To better understand the makeup of Bosnian names, we should understand the history of this land. Bosnia was part of the Ottoman Empire from the mid-15th century until late 19th century. The Ottomans brought Islam to the people and influenced the cultural and social fabric of the communities in this region. Although in 1878, Bosnia and Herzegovina fell under the Austro-Hungarian rule and remained so until World War I, the Ottomans continued to maintain a presence there. During the interbellum period that followed, Bosnia became part of the Kingdom of Yugoslavia, and after World War II it was granted full republic status in the Social Federal Republic of Yugoslavia. After the dissolution of Yugoslavia in 1992, Bosnia and Herzegovina became an independent nation. Slightly more than half of its population is Muslim. The Bosnian language is the standardized variety of Serbo-Croatian (Pickering et al, n.d.). This medley of languages and customs left its mark on Bosnian surname patterns, which reflect the influence of Turkish, as well as Arabic and Persian names and vocabulary. Yet, a large majority of Bosnian surnames carry the suffix *-ić*, as do the other South Slavic surnames. Aside from many of the surname patterns Bosnians share with other Serbo-Croatians, the influence of more than four centuries under Ottoman rule cannot be denied, as can be seen in most of the following examples.

Patronymic surnames

- Bektešević – offspring of Bektaş
- Džaferović – offspring of Džafer, Bosnian form of Arabic Jafar
- Ferhatović – offspring of Ferhat, Turkish form of Old Persian Farhad
- Habibović – offspring of Habib, Arabic for *beloved*
- Mehmedović – offspring of Mehmet, Turkish form of Arabic Mohammed

Occupational surnames

- Bajractarević – flag bearer (from Turkish *bajractar*)
- Čeliković – steelworker (from Serbo-Croatian *čelik* /Turkish *çelik* = steel + *-ović*,
- patronym)
- Demić – iron worker (from Turkish *demir* = iron)
- Ekmečić – baker (Serbian and Bosnian forms of Turkish *ekmekçi*)
- Galijašević – galley worker; also a toponymic, man from Gaul (*galija* = galley, Gaul)
- Hodžić – master, teacher, imam (*hodža*, word of Persian origin)
- Terzić – tailor (*terzija*, of Persian origin)

Descriptive surnames (nouns)

- Begić – chieftain, lord (*beg*, from Ottoman Turkish *bey*)
- Delić – brave man, soldier (who fought for the Ottoman Empire)
- Hadžić – someone who has completed the *hadž* (*hajj* = pilgrimage to Mecca, Arabic)
- Harambašić – senior commander of a band of bandits (*hajduks*) who fought for the Ottomans in the Balkans (*haranbaša*, Bosnian and Serbo-Croatian)

Habitational / Toponymic surnames

- Granov – from Granov, Ukraine (short form of Granovsky)
- Gusinjac – from Gusinje, town in Montenegro where Bosnians form a majority

Nicknames derived from **nature**

- Bilbija – nightingale (from *bilbil*, Serbo-Croatian variant of Turkish *bülbül*)
- Guli – flower, rose (Persian)
- Mišić – small mouse/muscle, from given name Mišo (also Serbo-Croatian)

The 10 most common surnames in Bosnia and Herzegovina are (Forebears, 2012-2022h):

1. **Hodžić** (master, teacher, imam – Turkish word of Persian origin)
2. **Kovačević** (blacksmith's offspring – Slavic surname)
3. **Marković** (offspring of Mark, the Roman god of war, plus the Slavic patronymic suffix)

4. **Petrović** (offspring of Peter – patronymic Southern Slavic surname)
5. **Tomić** (offspring of Toma/Tomas – patronymic Slavic surname)
6. **Delić** (brave man, soldier who fought for the Ottoman Empire)
7. **Hadžić** (someone who has completed the *hadž*; hajj = pilgrimage to Mecca, Arabic)
8. **Savić** (offspring of Sava – patronymic Slavic surname)
9. **Halilović** (offspring of Halil, Turkish form of Arabic Khalil)
10. **Babić** (offspring of an old woman – matronymic Slavic surname)

This list of the most common Bosnian surnames shows a fairly even distribution between Slavic and Turkish/Persian/Arabic name origins, a reflection of the ethnic makeup of the people of Bosnia and Herzegovina.

BULGARIAN

Bulgarian and Macedonian constitute the eastern group of Southern Slavs. Although Bulgaria is considered a South Slavic country, it is similar to the Eastern Slavic countries in its naming customs. Although separated geographically by non-Slavic Romania, they share the tripartite naming system of given name, patronymic middle name, and surname.

The patronymic second name is formed from the father's given name plus the suffix *-ov* or *–ev* for males and *-ova* or *-eva* for females. The surname is inherited from one's father and inflected for gender for daughters. Women traditionally have adopted their husband's last name upon marriage (adjusted for gender), but maintained their first and second names. So, for instance, if Elena Georgieva Nikolova married Ivan Borisov Zahariev, she would become Elena Georgieva Zaharieva and their children might be named Boris Ivanov Zahariev and Sofia Ivanova Zaharieva. Notice that, like Russian names, the feminine surname endings for 'daughter of' and 'wife of' are the same, but unlike Russian names, one cannot count on the patronymic second name to differentiate between them because the second name endings and the surname endings are identical. So if Elena Georgieva's name happened to be Elena Ivanova, since Ivan is a very common name, there would be no way of knowing if a woman named Ivanova Zaharieva was Ivan Borisov Zahariev's wife or daughter.

To add to this possible confusion, it has been customary to name a son after his paternal grandfather, so the tripartite name would repeat itself every other generation. So, Anton Bogdanov Vanchev's son would be named Bogdan Antonov Vanchev, and his son would be Anton Bogdanov Vanchev, and so on. Fortunately, naming customs have relaxed and today people are freer to choose their names and those of their children. A woman may choose to keep her maiden name, adopt her husband's or hyphenate the two. A husband is also free to choose between his and his wife's surname, and both parents can choose any name they like for their children. However, this doesn't mean that most people choose to ignore traditional naming customs just because the law allows it. These customs still govern their choices, especially in small towns and rural areas.

The most common surname suffixes are the patronymic ***-ov/-ova*** and ***-ev/-eva***, which are identical to the patronymic second name endings. Another group of much less common suffixes are ***-ski/-ska*** (or ***-ki/-ka***), which sometimes indicate geographical origin. For example, the surname Dobrudzhanski indicates that the family originates from Dobrudja, a region in northeastern Bulgaria on the Black Sea. The name Pernishki might place the origin of the family in the town of Pernik, in Western Bulgaria.

Since the masculine and feminine surnames are listed separately, we have expanded the list of the most common surnames to the top 20. The names on this list are strikingly uniform (National Statistical Institute [NSI], 2018). It isn't until numbers 35 and 38 on the list that we find Mehmed and Ahmed, two Muslim surnames. Sunni Muslims are the second-largest religious community after Eastern Orthodox, constituting 10% of the population, according to the 2011 census (NSI, 2011).

1. Ivanova
2. Ivanov
3. Georgieva
4. Georgiev
5. Dimitrova
6. Dimitrov
7. Petrova
8. Petrov
9. Nikolova
10. Nikolov
11. Hristova
12. Stoyanova
13. Todorova
14. Hristov
15. Stoyanov
16. Todorov
17. Ilieva
18. Angelova
19. Iliev
20. Angelov

MACEDONIAN

North Macedonia, one of the successor states of former Yugoslavia, is bordered by Greece, Albania, Kosovo, Serbia and Bulgaria. The official languages are Macedonian and Albanian. Macedonians are the largest ethnic group, making up almost two thirds of the population, followed by Albanians, who make up one quarter. Smaller ethnic groups are Turks, Romani, Serbs, Bosniaks, and Aromanians, who constitute about one tenth of the population and have their own official regional languages. Two thirds of the population are Christian, belonging to the Macedonian Eastern Orthodox Church, and one third are Muslim.

Most Macedonian surnames are formed by adding the patronymic suffix ***-ski*** to a given name, title or occupation, which sometimes already has the possessive suffix ***-ev***. In these cases, the two combine to form the endings ***-evski*** and ***-ovski***, often reduced to ***-eski*** and ***-oski***. Female surnames reflect the Eastern Slavic patterns of inflecting for grammatical gender: ***-ski*** to ***-ska***, ***-ev*** to ***-eva***, ***-ov*** to ***-ova***. Among ethnic Albanians or the Macedonians of Albania, most surnames do not have suffixes.

The 20 most common surnames in North Macedonia are (Forebears, 2012-2022i):

1. **Stojanovski**
2. **Jovanovska**
3. **Jovanovski**
4. **Stojanovska**
5. **Nikolovska**
6. **Nikolovski**
7. **Trajkovski**
8. **Stojanova**
9. **Trajkovska**
10. **Ramadani** (Albanian)
11. **Stojanov**
12. **Atanasova**
13. **Petrovska**
14. **Krstevski**
15. **Gjorgjievska**
16. **Ilievska**
17. **Jovanov**
18. **Krstevska**
19. **Bajrami** (Albanian)
20. **Atanasov**

Macedonians do not exhibit the diversity of surnames of the members of the western group of Southern Slavs. In fact, the most striking aspect of this list is the high percentage of patronymic surnames, containing the possessive suffixes ***-ov/-ova*** or the double suffixes ***-ovski/-ovska***, meaning 'offspring of'. Ramadani is an Albanian name, derived from the Arabic *Ramadan*, the ninth month of the Hijri year. Ramadanov is a Slavicized version of this name. Bajrami is also an Albanian name, derived from the Muslim holy day *Bayram*, a Turkic word originally from Middle Persian.

THE SOUTHERN BALKANS

The Balkan Peninsula, the area in southeastern Europe surrounding the Balkan Mountains in Bulgaria, is inhabited by a variety of ethnic, linguistic, and religious groups. There is no universal agreement as to its member nations. In its most inclusive sense, it consists of, in full or in part, the countries of Romania, Bulgaria, Albania, Greece and the independent states of the former Yugoslavia—Serbia, Croatia, Bosnia and Herzegovina, Slovenia, North Macedonia, and Montenegro. Many geographers, however, consider the northern border of the peninsula to be the Danube, thus excluding Romania and the northern part of Serbia. The European part of Turkey is sometimes included; in fact, it is interesting to note that the word *balkan* means 'chain of wooded mountains' in modern Turkish, a word derived from Persian. Of the countries whose entire territory is within the borders of the Balkans, the only ones not explored in the Southern Slavic section are Greece and Albania, so their surname traditions are examined here under The Southern Balkans.

GREEK

Surnames were not used in ancient Greece. Patronyms in the genitive case were added to clarify the identity of an individual. Occasionally, a third element was added to indicate a city of origin or membership in a kinship group. So Georgios Demetrides of Paiania was Georgios, son of Demetrios, originating from the city of Paiania.

Hereditary surnames began to be used by wealthy families in the 11th and 12th centuries. These names came from nicknames, occupations, or place names, rather than patronyms. Over the next few centuries, surname use gradually spread to other social classes, and by early 19th century, they became commonplace throughout Greece. By that time patronymic names had become the most widely used by all except the upper classes.

Greek names legally consist of a first name, a patronymic name, and a family name. The patronymic is the genitive form of the father's personal name, which means it usually carries the suffix *-ou* (of). Some common patronymics are Georgiou (offspring of Georgios), Antoniou (offspring of Antonis), Dimitriou/Demetriou (offspring of Dimitrios). Until recently, women changed their patronymic surnames from their father's to their husband's surname upon marriage by attaching the feminine form of the genitive suffix to the husband's first name. So, for example, if Eleni Ioannou Papadopoulous (daughter of Ioannis Papadopoulous) married Geórgios Evriviades, she would become Eleni Georgíou Evriviadou. If she became widowed, she would revert to her father's patronymic but retain her husband's surname to become Eleni Ioannou Evriviadou.

In modern times, Greek women keep their birth surname for life, although they have the option of adding their husband's surname to their own. In 1983, Greece enacted a gender equality law when it came to surnames in marriage. Both partners keep their birth names and, if they have children, they decide whether they will have the mother's or the father's last name, or both.

According to Forebears (n.d.), there are over 280,000 unique surnames in Greece, the most popular being Papadopoulos. Greek surnames are especially interesting because they provide a wealth of information for those wanting to learn more about their Greek ancestry. They tend to be long, although some have been abbreviated. The first part of the name, the prefix, is often derived from an occupation, such as Papa- (priest), Archi- (boss), Mastro- (craftsman), and can be combined with a patronymic suffix—Kapetanidis (offspring or descendent of a ship captain), Papadopoulos (offspring or descendant of a priest). Unlike Catholics, Greek Orthodox priests married and had families.

The majority of Greek surnames are patronymic. There are a variety of patronymic suffixes that, aside from indicating the relationship of offspring or descendant, also point to the place of origin of the family. Here are some of the most common **patronymic suffixes** and their **geographical origins:**

- ***-akis*** (Crete and the Aegean Islands)
- ***-atos*** (the island of Kefalonia)
- ***-opoulos*** (Peloponnesus)
- ***-idis, -ides, -iadis, -iades*** (Anatolia and Eastern Thrace, Pontus, Asia Minor, Messina, Lanonia)
- ***-ellis*** (Lesbos)
- ***-oudas*** (Macedonia)
- ***-oulis*** (Thessalia)
- ***-as*** (Macedonia and the Epirus)
- ***-eas*** (the Messenian part of the Mani peninsula)

Of the above suffixes, several are diminutives (***-akis, -oulis***), others indicate descent (***-idis, -ides, -iadis, -iades, -opoulos***), and yet others use a genitive marker to indicate possession (***-ou***).

At this point it bears clarifying the difference between the patronymic second name and the patronymic surname. The second name is based on an individual's father's first name, bearing the genitive suffix *-ou*, meaning 'offspring of'. It changes from generation to generation. On the other hand, the surname is passed on unchanged to the next generation. It is not derived from a person's father's name, but rather from an ancestor. Most Greek surnames end in *-s*, which is the masculine ending for proper nouns in the nominative case. Some, though, use the genitive ending ***-ou***.

Aside from patronymic suffixes, surnames can also reflect a person's or family's place of origin.

- Aivaliotis – from Ayvalik, a Turkish town
- Arvanitis – Albanian
- Kritikos – from Crete
- Kritikos, Kypros and its variants Kypraios, Kypraiou, Kypriadis, Kypriotakis, Kyprizoglou – from Cyprus
- Nisiotis – from the islands

- Thessalonikios – from Thessalonika

Surnames ending in ***-oglou*** are of Turkish origin, so Kyprizoglou would likely belong to a family of Turkish descent from Cyprus.

Another combination of **patronymic geographical** surnames point to the country of origin of the family.

- Frangopoulos – French, Frank
- Persopoulos – Persian
- Rousopoulos – Russian
- Servopoulos – Serbian
- Voulgaropoulos – Bulgarian

Occupational surnames can refer to an ancestor's trade or occupation, such as:

- Ganas – coppersmith
- Hasapis – butcher
- Kaffetzis – coffee house owner
- Kaltsis – stockings salesman
- Loukanis – sausage maker
- Metaxas – silk merchant
- Mylonas – miller
- Papas – priest
- Papoutsis – shoemaker
- Raptis – tailor
- Samaras – saddle maker

The suffixes ***-tzis/-tsis*** also denote an occupation, much as the suffix *-er* does in English.

A large group of Greek surnames are **descriptive** of a physical characteristic or a personality trait.

- Galanis – blue-eyed
- Hondros – fat
- Kallis – best
- Kappas – large
- Katsaros – curly
- Kokkinis – red
- Kontos – short
- Koufos – deaf
- Koutsos – lame

- Leventis – brave
- Makris – long, tall
- Markos – clever
- Mauros – black, dark
- Mytaras – large-nosed
- Nanos – dwarf
- Spanos – beardless
- Xanthakos – blond

Many adjectives are used as prefixes. Here is are some common ones:

- Archi- – boss
- Gero- – old, wise
- Hadji- – Arabic word referring to someone who has made the pilgrimage to Mecca
- Hondro- – fat
- Kara- – black
- Konto- – short
- Makro- – tall
- Mastro- – mason, worker
- Palaio- – old

Foreign terms modified into Greek surnames also point to a country of origin. A large number of them come from Turkish words, such as:

- Bakirtzis – coppersmith
- Karas – black
- Katsakis – fugitive or escapee
- Paras – money
- Sarris – blond, fair-headed

Some surnames come from **animal names.**

- Aetos – eagle
- Gataki – kitten
- Leos – lion
- Lykaios – wolf
- Matsouka – bat
- Tsaoussis – peacock
- Vouvali – buffalo
- Xiphias – swordfish

The 10 most common Greek surnames are (Chrysopoulos, 2021):

1. **Papadopoulos** (offspring of the priest)
2. **Pappas** (priest)
3. **Karagiannis** (black-haired Giannis)
4. **Vlahos, Vlachos** (ethnic name for Vlachs, Romance-speaking peoples of the Balkans)
5. **Ioannidis** (offspring of Ioannis)
6. **Economou** (of the housekeeper, accountant, steward)
7. **Papageorgiou** (offspring of Father George)
8. **Makris** (long, tall)
9. **Konstantinidis** (offspring of Konstantinos)
10. **Dimopoulos** (offspring of Dimos)

The island country of CYPRUS in the Eastern Mediterranean has two official languages: Greek and Turkish. Greek Cypriots comprise almost four fifths of the country's population. The top 10 most common surnames in Cyprus are Greek (Forebears, 2012-2022j).

1. **Georgiou** (offspring of Giorgios)
2. **Charalambous** (from the personal name *Charalampos* – *χαρά* (*chara*)=happiness + *λάμπω* (*lampo*)=to shine
3. **Ioannou** (offspring of Ioannes)
4. **Constantinou** (offspring of Konstantinos)
5. **Christodoulou** (servant of Christ)
6. **Demetriou** (follower of Demetrios, goddess of fertility)
7. **Michael** (derivation from personal name Michalis, originally from Hebrew *Mikha'el*=who is like God)
8. **Nicolaou** (offspring of Nikolaos)
9. **Andreou** (offspring of Andreas)
10. **Antoniou** (offspring of Antonios)

ALBANIAN

Albania has been a secular country with no official religion not only since the beginning of the Communist regime in 1944, but for much of the 20th century. Many people saw religion as a dividing, rather than a unifying force in a country made up of Sunni Muslims (50%), Orthodox Christians (20%), Bektashi Muslims (20%), and Roman Catholics (10%). Any form of religious observance was not only discouraged, but punished. As a result, interfaith marriages between Muslims and Christians were common. In the post-Communist era, these policies were abandoned and freedom of religion was extended to all citizens. Consequently, some people of Muslim ancestry began to practice Christianity and some Christians converted to Islam. All these factors led to an interesting phenomenon. Many Albanians have surnames with Islamic or Christian roots that often do not match their actual religious identity. And when people speak about their religious identity, they refer to their ancestral traditions rather than their own religious beliefs.

Albanians are in the majority in Albania and Kosovo, and they form the largest ethnic minority in North Macedonia. Smaller ethnic minorities inhabit Montenegro, Serbia, Croatia, as well as Greece, Italy and Turkey.

Full Albanian names consist of a given name, the given name of the father (usually only included in official documents) and a family name. Most family names in Albania are patronymic—with Islamic or Christian roots or derived from old Albanian secular names—or they are derived from clan names or place names. A majority of surnames end in vowels: -*aj* (*j* is a vocalic sound similar to *i*), *-i, -u, -a/-ja.*

Patronymic surnames of Islamic descent derived from Turkish given names

- Abazi – from Abbas
- Ahmeti, Ahmetaj – from Ahmed, Ahmet
- Brahimi – from Ibrahim
- Halili – from Halil
- Hasani – from Hasan
- Islami – from Islam
- Mehmeti, Mehmedi – from Mehmet, Mehmed
- Mustafi – from Mustafa
- Rahmani – from Rahmi (Arabic *Rahman*)
- Ramadani – from Ramazan (Arabic *Ramad*)

- Selimi – from Selim (Arabic *Salim*)
- Shaqiri – from Şakir (Arabic *Shakir*)

Patronymic surnames of Christian descent derived from given names, mostly from Greek

- Gjergji (George)
- Gjika, Gjoka (Jacob, Jake
- Gjoni, Gjonaj (John)
- Leka, Lekaj (Alex)
- Luka (Lucas)
- Marku (Mark)
- Nikolla (Nicholas)
- Thanasi (Athanasius)

Albanian surnames derived from secular names

- Dushku
- Rexhepi
- Shkoxa
- Zogolli

Albanian surnames derived from **clan names** are common in Northern Albania and Kosovo. Many of them are also toponymic, since the clan or tribe often takes its name from the region of origin.

- Berisha – one of the oldest documented Albanian tribes from northern Albania, southern Montenegro and Kosovo
- Bytyçi/Bytyqi – tribe from the Gjakova highlands
- Gashi – a major historical tribe from the District of Tropojë in northern Albania
- Gjika (Romanian *Ghica*) – noble family of Wallachia, Moldavia, and the Kingdom of Romania from 17th to 19th century
- Gjokaj – Albanian surname of the Triesh clan of Malësia region of southern Montenegro
- Gjoni/Gjonaj – Albanian clan in northern Albania and Montenegro
- Hoti – historical Albanian tribe and sub-region of Malësia, a divided area in northern Albania and southern Montenegro
- Kastrati – tribe of the Malësi e Madhe area in northern Albania
- Kelmendi – historical Albanian tribe in Malësia, in eastern Montenegro

- Krasniqi – a tribe of two different patrilineal ancestries from Kolë Mekshi from the 16th century
- Morina – small tribe and historical region of the Gjakova highlands in Kosovo
- Shala – historical tribe and region of northern Albania
- Shkreli – historical tribe and region in the Malësia Madhe region of northern Albania
- Thaçi/Thaqi – historical Albanian tribe and region in northern Albania, believed to be originally from present day Montenegro

Toponymic surnames may denote a former residence of a family, as they moved from place to place.

- Delvina – from a district in southern Albania before 2000
- Dibra – from Debar, city in Macedonia
- Durrsaku – from Durrës County, in northern Albania
- Frashëri – from Frashër, a village in the Gjirokaster County, southern Albania
- Kavaja – from Kavajë, municipality in the Western Lowlands region of Albania
- Koroveshi – from a city in south-central Albania
- Kryeziu – from a small village in northern Albania (meaning *black headed*)
- Laci – from Laç, town in northwestern Albania
- Peja – from the región of Rugova, in western Kosovo
- Përmeti – from Përmet, town in southern Albania
- Prishtina – from the capital of Kosovo
- Rashica – from Rašica, a village in southern Serbia
- Rugova – from Rugova/Rugovë, a mountainous region in Kosovo
- Shkodra – from Shkodër, the largest city in northern Albania

Occupational names are rare in Albania. Ironically, the most common ones relate to religious figures, which happen to make up four of the 10 most common family names in Albania (Bazaj, 2013).

1. **Hoxha** and its variant **Hoxhaj** (Imam, Muslim religious leader, Sunni or Bektashi)
2. **Shehu** (Bektashi priest, possibly derived from 'sheikh')
3. **Prifti** (Orthodox or Catholic priest)
4. **Çela, Çelaj** (patronymic from given name)

5. **Leka, Lekaj** (patronymic from given name equivalent to Alex)
6. **Dervishi** (Bektashi priest)
7. **Hysi** (toponymic from nickname of Hussein)
8. **Rama** (patronymic from nickname of Ramazan)
9. **Dibra** (toponymic from Debar, city in Macedonia)
10. **Abazi** (patronymic from given name Abbas)

TWO MORE

Romanian, Moldovan and Hungarian are not Slavic languages, so they do not fit neatly into any of the categories of Slavic people examined so far. Romanian and Moldovan are very closely related Romance languages, and Hungarian is one of a small group of non-Indo-European languages spoken in Europe, which includes Finnish, Estonian and Basque.

ROMANIAN

Before the 19th century, Romanian names consisted of a given name, followed by the father's name and the grandfather's name. After the family name reform was introduced in mid-19th century, people's names were modified to align with Western European names, consisting of a given name, occasionally a second given name or middle name, and a family name. The family name was passed on patrilineally and usually women adopted their husband's name upon marriage. When paternity was not established, a descendant took the mother's surname. Nowadays the law is flexible and gives couples the right to choose their family name, which would also be given to their descendants. They may choose to use either one of their surnames or to hyphenate them. If parents have different surnames, the descendants have to have either one or both of their parents' surnames.

The overwhelming majority of Romanian surnames end in ***-u***, a reduced form of the suffix *-ul*, which is the definite masculine singular article, so it adds the meaning 'the one who' to the rest of the appellation. Thus, Rusu would mean the 'Russian one', Moldoveanu 'the one from Moldova', Croitoru 'the tailor', Barbu 'the bearded one', and so on. It is possible that in their earliest versions, these names contained the full suffix *-ul* and were later reduced. Since the *-l* is not usually pronounced, it makes sense that it would be elided.

Romanian family names fall under the usual principal categories.

Patronymic surnames

The suffix ***-escu*** (or less commonly, ***-aşcu*** or ***-ăscu***) is added to a male ancestor's given name as a possessive adjective. Cognates include Romanian *-esc*, Latin *-iscus*, Italian *-isco*, French *-esque*, English *-ish*.

- Alexandrescu – descendant of Alexandru
- Dumitrescu – descendant of Dumitru
- Ionescu – descendant of Ion (John)
- Petrescu, Petraşcu, Pătraşcu – descendant of Petre (Peter)
- Popescu – descendant of a priest (also Popovici, Serbo-Croatian origin)
- Rădulescu – descendant of Radu

Geographical (toponymic or **topographic)** surnames

The suffixes ***-eanu***, ***-anu*** or ***-an*** added to a place (river, city/village, region or country) usually indicate a place of origin of the family (cognate to Italian *(i)ano*). The *-u* ending is reduced from *-ul*, the definite masculine singular article, adding the meaning 'the one who is from...'.

- Ardeleanu – from the Ardeal region of Transylvania
- Moldoveanu – from Moldova
- Munteanu – from the mountains
- Rusu, Rusianu – from Russia
- Sadoveanu – from the commune Sadova, in Suceava county
- Ungureanu – from Hungary

Occupational surnames often end in the suffixes ***-aru, -oru, -anu.*** Here too, the ending *-u*, reduced from *-ul*, adds the meaning 'the one who' has that occupation.

- Ciobanu / Păcuraru – shepherd
- Ciubotaru, Ciobotaru – boot maker
- Cojocaru – sheepskin coat maker
- Croitoru – tailor
- Dascălu – teacher
- Fieraru – smith
- Funaru – ropemaker
- Moraru – miller
- Popa – priest
- Pușcașu – gunsmith (cognate of the Hungarian name *Puskás*, from *puska*, meaning *gun*)
- Văcaru – cowherd; also the patronym Văcărescu (descendant of a cowheard)

Descriptive surnames derived from **nicknames**

The suffix *-u* in this category adds the meaning 'the one who is...'.

- Albu – white
- Barbu – bushy beard; also the patronym Bărbulescu (descendant of a bearded man)
- Bălan – blond
- Crețu – curly haired
- Grosu – stout, bulky
- Lungu – long, tall

- Roșu – red
- Negru, Negreanu, Negrescu – black

Surnames derived from **animals**

The suffix *-u* in this category adds the meaning 'the one who looks like a(n)...'.

- Boureanu – ox (*bou*)
- Căpreanu – goat (*capra*)
- Ciuraru – crow (*cioara*)
- Jderoiu – marten (*jder*)
- Lupu – wolf (*lup*)
- Ursu – bear (*urs*)
- Vulpe – fox

Surnames from **given names**

- Dumitru, Dumitriu
- Gheorghe
- Luca
- Matei
- Radu
- Șerban
- Stan, Stancu
- Ștefan
- Stoian
- Vlad

The 10 most common Romanian surnames according to Forebears (2012-2022k) are:

1. **Popa** (priest)
2. **Popescu** (descendant of a priest)
3. **Pop** (short for Popa)
4. **Radu** (from the given name Radu, of Slavic origin, meaning *happy*)
5. **Dumitru** (from the given name Dumitru, derived from the Greek *Demetrius*)
6. **Stan** (short for Stanislav, given name of Slavic origin)
7. **Stoica** (possibly meaning *stoic*)
8. **Gheorghe** (from the given name Gheorghe, a form of *George*)
9. **Matei** (from the given name Matei, Romanian for *Matthew*)
10. **Rusu** (the Russian)

MOLDOVAN (Moldavian) is the variety of Romanian spoken in the Republic of Moldova, a sovereign state in Eastern Europe between Romania and Ukraine. It was an integral part of Romania until 1812, after which time it switched back and forth several times between Russia and Romania until it became an independent nation in 1991. The similarity of Moldovan to Romanian is reflected in the names of its people.

The 10 most common surnames in Moldova according to Forebears (2012-2022l) are:

1. **Rusu** (the Russian)
2. **Ceban** (shepherd)
3. **Ciobanu** (the shepherd)
4. **Lungu** (the long/tall one)
5. **Cebotari** (shoemaker)
6. **Munteanu** (from the mountain)
7. **Popa** (the priest)
8. **Guţu** (diminutive form of *Gheorghe* or *Grigore*)
9. **Rotari** (wheelwright, from *roată*=wheel)
10. **Balan** (blonde)

HUNGARIAN

Hungarian names follow the Eastern name order, like the Chinese, Japanese, Korean and Vietnamese, in which the family name is followed by the given name. When asked to explain this peculiarity for a European country, a Hungarian might point to a general tendency in Hungary to follow the logical order of big to small (for dates, year – month – day; for addresses, country – city – street – house number – apartment number). The most important information comes from the first datum, then the field is narrowed down, much as telephone numbers are used all over the world (country code – city code – area code – number). Other countries in Eastern Europe also tend to use surnames first, not only in official documents, but also in school and work environments. However, this practice is not carried out in all facets of daily life and is not mandated by law, as it is in Hungary.

Once people marry, they have several options for the family name. Until the 18th century, noble women kept their names and their children took their father's surname. Women from other social classes took their husband's name. So if Farkas Ilona married Molnar Tamás, she would become Molnar Tamásné (the ***-né*** suffix means *wife of*). This law was in effect until 1952. During the Communist era, in an effort toward equality of the sexes, women were given the right to choose between keeping their name or taking their husband's (Splash, 2014). Over the next few decades, the options for women increased, so Ilona could choose any of the following:

- Keep her full birth name → Farkas Ilona
- Give up her name and add *-né* to her husband's full name → Molnar Tamásné. The name *Ilona* will no longer be part of her official name, but she will be called so informally.
- Add *-ne* to her husband's surname and keep her name → Molnarné Farkas Ilona
- Add *-ne* to her husband's full name and keep her name → Molnar Tamásné Farkas Ilona
- Take her husband's family name and keep her given name → Molnar Ilona

While this law gave a lot of options to women, it didn't to men, so it was declared sexist and unconstitutional until an amendment was added in 2004, listing the options for men. So Tamás could choose among the following:

- Keep his full birth name → Molnar Tamás
- Take his wife's family name and keep his given name → Farkas Tamás
- Hyphenate their family names in either order for either one of the spouses or both → Molnar-Farkas or Farkas-Molnar. If only one spouse uses a hyphenated name, the other must keep his or her original surname.

The decision about the chosen family name(s) is to be announced at the wedding, as is the choice for their future children's. All the children of the couple must have the same family name, which can be either parent's surname or a hyphenated one, as long as it is on the marriage certificate.

Same-sex marriages have not yet become legal in Hungary.

The most common categories of surnames are:

Occupational surnames

- Dudás – bagpipe player
- Erdös – forester
- Fazekas – potter
- Hajós – sailor
- Halász – fisherman
- Hegedűs – fiddler
- Juhász – shepherd
- Kalmár – merchant, shopkeeper
- Katona – soldier
- Kertész – gardener
- Kocsis – coachman
- Kovács – smith
- Lakatos – locksmith
- Mészáros – butcher
- Mészáros – butcher
- Molnár – miller
- Pap – priest
- Pék – baker
- Sipos – whistler, piper
- Szabó – tailor
- Szücs – furrier
- Takács – weaver
- Varga – shoemaker

Descriptive surnames (derived from nicknames)

- Arany – golden
- Balogh – left-handed
- Barma – brown
- Erös – strong
- Eszes – bright, clever
- Fehér – white
- Fekete – black
- Fodor – curly, wavy (hair)
- Kis, Kiss – little
- Kövér – fat
- Nagy – big

- Nemes – noble, gentle
- Szép – beautiful
- Szőke – blond
- Tar – bald
- Vastag – stout
- Vörös – red

Toponymic/topographic surnames

- Budai – from Buda
- Dunai – from Duna (the Danube)
- Kárpáti, Kárpáty – from Kárpáti (Carpathian Mountains)
- Pataki – someone who lives near a creek (*patak* = creek)
- Pesti, Pesty – from Pest
- Pusztai – someone living on a plain (*puszta* = plain)
- Sárközi, Sárközy, Sarkozi, Sarkozy – someone from Sárköz, a region in Hungary

Ethnic surnames

- Görög – Greek
- Horváth – Croat
- Lengyel – Pole
- Magyar – Hungarian
- Németh – German
- Oláh – Vlah/Romanian
- Olasz – Italian
- Orosz – Russian
- Rácz – Serb
- Török – Turk
- Tót, Tóth – Slovak or Slovene

Derivations from **animals**

- Bárány – lamb
- Farkas – wolf
- Sas – eagle
- Sólyom – hawk, falcon
- Szarka – magpie (euphemistic term for a thief)

Some might find it surprising not to find a category of patronymic surnames, which are so popular in most European countries. Instead, we find some limited uses of bynames. A byname is a type of non-inheritable name that is used to identify a specific individual. We've already seen the byname suffix ***-né***, which identifies a woman as being someone's wife. There is also the suffix ***-fi*** (an abbreviation of ***-fia***, meaning *son of*) and its variants ***-fia, -fy, -fÿ***, which signal a filial relationship, as in:

- Bertoldfia – son of Bertold
- Jákobfi – son of Jacob
- Laszlofi – son of Laszlo
- Petöfi – son of Petö, a diminutive of Péter
- Sándorfy – son of Sándor
- Zoltánfi – son of Zoltan

What would be classified as an inheritable patronymic surname would be one derived from **an ancestor's given name** or a diminutive of it.

- Fülöp
- Gábor
- Gáspár
- László
- Lukács
- Pál
- Péter
- Petö (old diminutive of Péter)
- Rózsa, Ruzsa (matronymic from the given name Rösza)
- Samsa (diminutive of Sámuel)
- Sándor

The 10 most frequent surnames in Hungary are (Budapest Agent, 2022):

1. **Nagy** (big)
2. **Kovács** (smith)
3. **Tóth** (Slavic, Slovak)
4. **Szabó** (tailor)
5. **Horváth** (Croat)
6. **Varga** (shoemaker)
7. **Kis** (small)

8. **Molnár** (miller)
9. **Németh** (German)
10. **Farkas** (wolf)

References

SOUTHERN AND WESTERN EUROPE

ITALIAN

Adams, S. R. (2018, August 13). *Italian last names: Their meaning, origin, and significance.* Family Search. https://www.familysearch.org/blog/en/my-italian-last-name/

Donati, S. (2022, February 10). *The interesting history of Italian last names.* Italy Magazine. https://www.italymagazine.com/featured-story/interesting-history-italian-last-names

Johnston, H. W. (1903). *The private life of the Romans.* Scott, Foresman and Company. https://www.forumromanum.org/life/johnston.html

SPANISH

Albaigès, J. M. (1995). Enciclopedia de los nombres propios [Encyclopedia of names]. Barcelona, Spain: Planeta.

Boletín Oficial del Estado. (1999, November 6). Ley 40/1999, de 5 de noviembre, sobre nombre y apellidos y orden de los mismos. [Law 40/1999, November 5, on first and last names and order thereof]. https://www.boe.es/eli/es/l/1999/11/05/40/dof/spa/pdf

Buber (2020, August 16). Basque fact of the week: Basque surnames. https://buber.net/Basque/2020/08/16/basque-fact-of-the-week-basque-surnames/

El Almanaque. (n.d.). Léxico-Etimologías-Origen de las palabras-Expósito [Lexicon-Etymology-Word Origins-Expósito]. http://www.elalmanaque.com/lexico/exposito.htm

Europa Press. *(2017,* May 30). *El apellido del padre dejará definitivamente de tener preferencia en España a partir del 30 de junio* [The father's surname will no longer have preference in Spain starting June 30]. Madrid, Spain: *El Mundo,* 1. https://www.elmundo.es/sociedad/2017/05/30/592dba4d268e3e44738b476a.html

Europa Press. (2021, December 9). *Nombres y apellidos más frecuentes en España, según el INE* [The most frequent first and last names in Spain, according to the INE]. National Institute of Statistics. https://www.epdata.es/datos/nombres-apellidos-mas-frecuentes-espana-ine/373

Lang, L. (2014, September 17). *Family history, most popular, surnames.* https://blogs.ancestry.com/cm/4-types-of-spanish-surnames-which-one-is-yours/

Powell, K. (2019, July 12). *Garcia: Name meaning and origin.* ThoughtCo. https://www.thoughtco.com/garcia-last-name-meaning-and-origin-1422510

Solé-Morata, N., Bertranpetit, J., Comas, D., & Calafell, F. (2015). Y-chromosome diversity in Catalan surname samples: insights into surname origin and frequency. *European Journal of Human Genetics, 23*(11), 1549-1557. https://doi.org/10.1038/ejhg.2015.14

Wagadugu (2006, January 20). *Pronunciation of Catalan surnames in other languages.* Proz.com. https://www.proz.com/forum/pronunciation/41559-pronunciation_of_catalan_surnames_in_other_languages.html

PORTUGUESE

Catarina (2018, January 18). *What's in a name? Understanding the art of Portuguese names.* A Portuguese affair. https://www.aportugueseaffair.com/portuguese-names

Forebears. (2012-2022a). *Most common last names in Brazil.* https://forebears.io/brazil/surnames

Forebears. (2012-2022b). *Most common last names in Portugal.* https://forebears.io/portugal/surnames

FRENCH

Alister (2014, 23 December). *Evolution of family names in France.* France-Pub.com. https://www.france-pub.com/forum/2014/12/23/evolution-family-names-france/

Family Education. (2022, February 23). *French last names.* https://www.familyeducation.com/baby-names/browse-origin/surname/french

Forez. (n.d.). *Enfants abandonnés* [Abandoned children] – The patronymic given to foundlings, reflection of the attitude of society. http://forezhistoire.free.fr/enfants-trouves-e.html

Geopatronyme. (n.d.a) *Les noms de famille les plus portés par naissance en France entre 1891 et 1990.* [The most common surnames of those born in France between 1891 and 1990.] http://www.geopatronyme.com/cgi-bin/carte/hitnom.cgi?periode=5

Geopatronyme. (n.d.b) *Les noms de famille les plus portés par naissance en France entre 1966 et 1990.* [The most common surnames of those born in France between 1966 and 1990.] (n.d.) *geopatronyme.com.* http://www.geopatronyme.com/cgi-bin/carte/hitnom.cgi?periode=4

Guinness World Records. (2020, January 22). *Largest number of surnames.* https://www.guinnessworldrecords.com/world-records/largest-number-of-surnames/

Légifrance. (2021, August 4). *Des règles de devolution du nom de famille.* [Rules for the devolution of the surname]. Article 311-21. Code civil. https://www.legifrance.gouv.fr/codes/article_lc/LEGIARTI000027432045

BELGIAN

Hoitink, Y. (2013a, August 13). Dutch term: tussenvoegsel. Dutch Genealogy. https://www.dutchgenealogy.nl/tussenvoegsel/

Statbel. (n.d.). *Noms de famille les plus fréquents en 2021 – Belgique et Régions.* [Most common surnames in 2021 – Belgium and Regions]. https://statbel.fgov.be/fr/themes/population/noms-et-prenoms/noms-de-famille - figures

DUTCH

CBG (Center for Family History). (n.d.). *Database of surnames in the Netherlands.* https://www.cbgfamilienamen.nl/nfb/index.php?taal=eng

Hoitink, Y. (2005, August 11). Suffixes in surnames. Dutch Genealogy. https://www.dutchgenealogy.nl/suffixes-in-surnames/

Hoitink, Y. (2013a, August 13). Dutch term: tussenvoegsel. Dutch Genealogy. https://www.dutchgenealogy.nl/tussenvoegsel/

Hoitink, Y. (2013b, August 16). *Top 10 most common Dutch surnames.* Dutch Genealogy. https://www.dutchgenealogy.nl/popular-dutch-surnames/

Schulze, L. M. (2008, March 4). *Dutch patronymics of the 1600s.* New Netherland, New York Genealogy. Olive Tree Genealogy. http://www.olivetreegenealogy.com/nn/pat.shtml

The Netherlands by numbers. (2013, June 5). *14 Dutch surnames which you are glad are not yours.* https://netherlandsbynumbers.com/2013/06/05/14-dutch-surnames-which-you-are-

GERMAN

Alpenwild. (n.d.). *Common Swiss surnames and their origin.* https://www.alpenwild.com/staticpage/common-swiss-surnames-their-origin/

Born, S. (2015, February). *A piece of history: German surnames.* Alumniportal Deutschland. https://www.alumniportal-deutschland.org/en/germany/country-people/german-surnames-family-names/

Forebears. (2012-2022c). *Most common last names in Austria.* https://forebears.io/austria/surnames

Forebears. (2012-2022d). *Most common last names in Germany.* https://forebears.io/germany/surnames

Forebears. (2012-2022e). *Most common last names in Switzerland.* https://forebears.io/switzerland/surnames

Schochenmaier, E. (2018, March). *Preliminary study of the most frequent Russian, French and German occupational surnames.*

ResearchGate. https://www.researchgate.net/figure/Percentages-of-occupational-surnames-from-Germany-France-and-Russia_fig2_323737194

THE BRITISH ISLES

ENGLISH

Embury-Dennis, T. (2016, November 18). *The 25 most common surnames in Britain - and what they say about your family history.* The Independent. https://www.independent.co.uk/news/uk/home-news/the-25-common-surnames-britain-family-history-university-west-england-bristol-uk-a7423196.html

WELSH

Cooper, J. (2020, March 21). *The 50 most common Welsh surnames and how many of you have them.* WalesOnline. https://www.walesonline.co.uk/lifestyle/fun-stuff/50-most-common-welsh-surnames-17960729

SCOTTISH

National Records of Scotland (2020). *List of data tables. Most common surnames.* https://www.nrscotland.gov.uk/statistics-and-data/statistics/statistics-by-theme/vital-events/names/most-common-surnames/list-of-data-tables

IRISH

IrishCentral. (2021, September 3). *The official top 10 Irish surnames – is yours one of them?* https://www.irishcentral.com/roots/top-10-irish-surname

Woulfe, P. Rev. (1923). *Irish names and surnames. Anglicisation of Irish surnames.* Library Ireland. https://www.libraryireland.com/names/anglicisation-irish-surnames.php

The Nordic Countries

Ancestral Findings. (n.d.). *The meaning of your Scandinavian surname.* https://ancestralfindings.com/the-meaning-of-your-scandinavian-surname/

Norman, R. T. (n.d.). *Where is Scandinavia? A guide to the Scandinavian countries.* Scandinavia Standard. https://www.scandinaviastandard.com/where-is-scandinavia-a-guide-to-the-scandinavian-countries/

ICELANDIC

Carter, R. (n.d.) *Icelanding surnames: Exploring common Icelandic last names.* Scandification. https://scandification.com/icelandic-surnames-common-icelandic-last-names/

Hauksdóttir, G. (2016, January 29). *A nation on a first name basis. The Icelandic system explained.* ICENEWS. https://www.icenews.is/2016/01/29/a-nation-on-a-first-name-bases-the-icelandic-naming-system-explained/

Statistics Iceland. (2018, February 26). *Mannanöfn og nafngiftir á Íslandi* [Icelandic names and naming practice], *103*(3), 12. ..\..\..\Downloads\download.pdf https://hagstofan.s3.amazonaws.com/media/public/4a70b304-09ff-4c6b-adcf-050ac2bef384/pub_doc_5jMAKuA.pdf

DANISH

Fryxell, D. A. (n.d.). *Genealogy Q&A: Danish surnames.* Family Tree. https://www.familytreemagazine.com/names/surnames/danish-surnames-now-what/

Statista. (2022a). *Most common surnames in Denmark.* https://www.statista.com/statistics/745971/most-common-surnames-in-denmark/

NORWEGIAN

FamilySearch. (2022, March 18). *Norway personal names.* https://www.familysearch.org/en/wiki/index.php?title=Norway_Personal_Names&oldid=4689712

Rasin, L. (2020, November 4). *The most common Norwegian last names: An overview.* Norway Today. https://norwaytoday.info/everyday/the-most-common-norwegian-last-names-an-overview/

SWEDISH

Ahrholdt, J. (2004-2022a). *Nobility name.* Nordic Names. https://www.nordicnames.de/wiki/Nobility_Name

Ahrholdt, J. (2004-2022b). *Ornamental name.* Nordic Names. https://www.nordicnames.de/wiki/Ornamental_Name

Kamann, M. (2021, January 29). *Top 100 most common Swedish surnames: -son, -quist, -ström & Co.* (2019). Hej Sweden. https://hejsweden.com/en/swedish-surnames/

Olsson, N. W. (1981, March 1). What's in a Swedish surname? *Swedish American Genealogist, 1*(1), art. 15, 26-36. https://digitalcommons.augustana.edu/cgi/viewcontent.cgi?article=1292&context=swensonsag

FINNISH

Statista. (2022b). *Most common surnames in Finland.* https://www.statista.com/statistics/1017219/most-common-surnames-finland/

Stief, C. (2019, August 11). *Slash and burn agriculture explained.* ThoughtCo. https://www.thoughtco.com/slash-and-burn-agriculture-p2-1435798

Wallius, A. (2019, January 1). *The revised Name Act allows for four names and also brings international echoes to surnames.* Yle. https://yle.fi/uutiset/3-10576174

The Baltic States

ESTONIAN

Lestal, T. (2014, April 6). *The origin of Estonian surnames.* Estonia-Paradise of the North. http://estonia-paradise-of-the-north.blogspot.com/2014/04/the-origin-of-estonian-surnames.html

Raun, T. U. (2012). The movement to Estonianize surnames in interwar Estonia. *Acta Historica Tallinnensia, 18*(1), 97–107. doi: 10.3176/hist.2012.1.04

Surnam. (2022a). *Estonian surnames. Most common family names from Estonia*. https://surnam.es/estonia

LATVIAN

LSM. (2020, September 12). *Why did Latvians choose German surnames?* Public Broadcasting of Latvia. https://eng.lsm.lv/article/culture/history/why-did-latvians-choose-german-surnames.a374014/

Mawhood, W. (2016, September 23). *Why you will almost definitely have to change your name when speaking latvian.* Deep Baltic. https://deepbaltic.com/2016/09/23/why-you-will-almost-definitely-have-to-change-your-name-when-speaking-latvian/

Surnam. (2022b). *Latvian surnames. The most common Latvian surnames.* https://surnam.es/latvia

LITHUANIAN

Forebears. (2012-2022f). *Most common last names in Lithuania.* https://forebears.io/lithuania/surnames

Kudirka, J. (1991). *The Lithuanians. Lithuanian surnames.* Lithuanian Folk Culture Centre. http://www.lnkc.lt/eknygos/thelt/node9.html

THE SLAVIC COUNTRIES

EASTERN SLAVIC

RUSSIAN

Alexey. (2013-2019). *Top 20 most common Russian family names and their meanings.* ToDiscoverRussia. https://todiscoverrussia.com/top-20-most-common-russian-family-names-and-their-meaning/

UKRAINIAN

Forebears. (2012-2022g). *Most common last names in Ukraine.* https://forebears.io/ukraine/surnames

Slavutych, Y. (1962, September 1). Ukrainian surnames in -*enko. Names. 10* (3), 181–186. doi:10.1179/nam.1962.10.3.181. ISSN 0027-7738

BELARUSIAN

WorldNames. (2020). *The most common surnames in Belarus.* https://ru-worldnames-xyz.translate.goog/names/in-belarus/

WESTERN SLAVIC

CZECH

Lednicka B. (2014, January 31). *Most common Czech surnames.* Czech Genealogy for Beginners. http://czechgenealogy.nase-koreny.cz/2014/01/most-common-czech-surnames.html

SLOVAK

Jano. (2022). *What are some common Slovak last names?* Little Big Slovakia. https://littlebigslovakia.com/what-are-common-slovak-last-names-and-popular-surnames/

POLISH

Czarnecka, J. (2020, February 7). *10 most common surnames in Poland.* Careers in Poland. https://www.careersinpoland.com/article/people-and-relations/most-common-surnames-in-poland

Southern Slavic

SLOVENIAN

Borovnik, K. (2020, April 21). *Why do some Slovenians' surnames end in -ič while for the rest of the South Slavs surnames end in -ić?* Retrieved from Quora. https://www.quora.com/Why-do-some-Slovenians-surname-end-in-i%C4%8D-while-for-the-rest-of-the-South-Slavs-surnames-end-in-i%C4%87

Republic of Slovenia Statistical Office. (2021, January 1). *Top 100 family names.* https://www.stat.si/ImenaRojstva/en -/names/topLastnames

SERBO-CROATIAN

CroatiaWeek. (2020, November 7). *The 200 most common Croatian surnames.* https://www.croatiaweek.com/the-200-most-common-croatian-surnames/

Kursar, V. (2022, January 17). *13 popular Serbian last names: A painless guide.* Serbian Blog. https://ling-app.com/sr/serbian-last-names/

BOSNIAN

Forebears. (2012-2022h). *Most common last names in Bosnia and Herzegovina.* https://forebears.io/bosnia/surnames

Pickering, P., Malcolm, N. R. & Lampe, J. R. (n.d.). *Bosnia and Herzegovina.* In *Encyclopedia Britannica*. Retrieved from https://www.britannica.com/place/Bosnia-and-Herzegovina.

BULGARIAN

Republic of Bulgaria National Statistical Institute. (2011). *2011 Population census.* https://www.nsi.bg/census2011/PDOCS2/Census2011final_en.pdf

Republic of Bulgaria National Statistical Institute. (2018). *The most popular surnames.* https://www.nsi.bg/sites/default/files/files/pressreleases/Names2018p_en.pdf

MACEDONIAN

Forebears. (2012-2022i). *Most common last names in Macedonia.* https://forebears.io/north-macedonia/surnames

THE SOUTHERN BALKANS

GREEK

Chrysopoulos, P. (2021, March 4). *The 20 most common Greek last names*. Greek Reporter. https://greekreporter.com/2021/03/04/most-common-greek-last-names-greece/

Forebears. (2012-2022j). *Most common last names in Cyprus.* https://forebears.io/cyprus/surnames

ALBANIAN

Bazaj, I. (2013, May 24-25). *Anthroponimes and patronymes with higher frequency in onomastic vocabulary.* The 1st International Conference on Research and Education – Challenges Toward the Future. University of Shkodra, Shkodra, Albania. http://konferenca.unishk.edu.al/icrae2013/icraecd2013/doc/788.pdf

Two more

ROMANIAN

Forebears. (2012-2022k). *Most common last names in Romania.* https://forebears.io/romania/surnames

Forebears. (2012-2022l). *Most common last names in Moldova.* https://forebears.io/moldova/surnames

HUNGARIAN

Budapest Agent. (2022, June 8). *Most common Hungarian surnames.* http://www.budapestagent.com/most-common-hungarian-surnames.html

Splash-db.eu. (2014). *Policy: Hungarian family act, the Act IV. 1952 on marriage, family, and guardianship ('the Family Act').* https://splash-db.eu/policydocument/hungarian-family-act-the-act-iv-1952-on-marriage-family-and-guardianship-the-family-act/

Appendix A. Common surname prefixes and suffixes by country

Note: The prefixes and suffixes that constitute a significant majority (usually at least 20%) are in bold.

REGION	Language/ Nationality	COMMON PREFIXES	COMMON SUFFIXES
Southern and Western Europe	Italian	*La, Lo, Da, De, Del, Della, Delle, Di*	*-ini, -ino, -etti, -etto, -allo, -ello, -illo, -one, -accio, -acco, -occo, -ucco, -ucci, -uccio, -aso, -asso, -elli, -ozzi, -uzzi, -ano, -ino, -ini, -ico, -isio, -isso, -izzo, -azzo, -one, -ione, -aglia, -aldo, -otto, -ani, -ano, -ese, -esi, -eri, -engo, -ingo, -esco, -isco, -aro, -tore*
	Spanish	*de*	***-ez**, -az, -is, -oz, -os*
	- Basque		*-iz, -etxea, -buru, -aga, -barria, -eta*
	- Catalan	*Ll-* (sometimes within the name)	*-uig/-oig/-ig, -sch, -ch, -ó*
	Portuguese	*de, da, do*	*-es, -eira/-eiro, -eia*
	French	*De, Du, Des, Le*	*-eau, -elot, -elin, -elle, -elet, -ier, -ent, -et, -as, -and* *-aux, -beau, -champ, -court, -eux, -mont, -val, -ville*
	Belgian	Flemish: ***Van**, Van der, Ver, De* French: *Du, De la, Des, Le, La*	Flemish: ***-s, -ens, -(s)sens**, -x* (after *k*) French: *-er, -ier, -ain, -eur, -ant, -on*

	Dutch	***Van, De, Van der,*** *Van De, Van't* *Te, Ter, Ten*	*-s, -se, -sen, -szen, -x* *-ena, -enga, -ing, -inga, -ink, -ma* *-borg, -hof, -huis, -kamp*
	German	*von*	***-er***, *-mann* *-kamp, -hof* (can also be prefixes) *-berg*
The British Isles	English	*Fitz-, Kil-*	*-s, -son, -by, -don, -ford, -ham, -ley, -ton, -all, -ell, -well, -wood, -bridge, -ridge, -brook, -cock, -dale, -field, -hart, -hill, -house, -worth, -wright, -ings, -kins, -land, -lin, -man, -more, -shaw, -shire, -smith, -stone, -wick, -born/-bourn, -borough/-boro*
	Scottish	*Mac, Mc, Nc, Vc*	*-son*
	Welsh	*ab, ap, verch (vch)*	*-s*
	Irish	*Mac/Mag, O', Gil-*	
Nordic	Icelandic		*-(s)**son**, -(s)**dóttir**, -(s)bur* (non-binary, since 2019)
	Danish		***-sen***, *-gaard*
	Norwegian		***-sen***/*-son*
	Swedish		***-(s)son***, *-kvist/-qvist, -strom, -berg*
	Finnish		***-nen***, *-lä*

<table>
<tr><td colspan="2" rowspan="3">Baltic</td><td>Estonian</td><td>-</td><td>-</td></tr>
<tr><td>Latvian</td><td></td><td>-s/-š,-is (males); -a, -e (females)</td></tr>
<tr><td>Lithuanian</td><td></td><td>-as, -(i)us, -is (males); -ienė, (married F)
-aitė, -ytė, -ūtė, -tė (single F)
-(i)ukas (young single M in small villages)
-ė (F, regardless of marital status)</td></tr>
<tr><td rowspan="6">Slavic</td><td rowspan="3">Eastern Slavic</td><td>Russian</td><td></td><td>-ov/-ova, -ev/-eva, -in/-ina (M/F)</td></tr>
<tr><td>Ukrainian</td><td></td><td>-enko, -chuk, -chak, -uk, -ik, -yk, -iuk, -vich/-vych, -ko, -yshyn/-ishyn, -sky/-ska, -ov/-ova, -ev/-eva</td></tr>
<tr><td>Belarusian</td><td></td><td>-ov/-ova, -ev/-eva, -vič, -ič, -ka, -enka, -ko, -enko, -ak, -onak, -yonak, -uk, -yuk, -čuk, -ienia, -ski/-skaya</td></tr>
<tr><td rowspan="3">Western Slavic</td><td>Czech</td><td></td><td>-ová (F), -ček (diminutive), -era, -ý, -ak, -ek, -ik, -ac, -ec, -ka, -eš, -il, -ota (augmentative)</td></tr>
<tr><td>Slovak</td><td></td><td>-ová (F), -ec, -ek, -ák, -ik, -ík, -ič, -áč, -na, -ka, -ár, -ý</td></tr>
<tr><td>Polish</td><td></td><td>-ski, -cki, -zki, -dzki (M)
-ska (F)
-czyk, -yk, -ik, -ak, -ka, -szczak, -czak, -ek, -wicz, -owicz, -ewicz
-owna, -anka (unmaried F)
-ina/-yna (married F)</td></tr>
</table>

	Southern Slavic	Slovenian		***-ič***, *-nik, -ar, -ec, -šek, -ko*
	Southern Slavic	Serbo-Croatian		**-ić**, -ar
	Southern Slavic	Bosnian		***-ić***
	Southern Slavic	Bulgarian		***-ov/-ova*, *-ev/-eva,*** *-ski/-ska, -ki/-ka* (M/F)
	Southern Slavic	Macedonian		***-ski/-ska, -ov/-ova, -ovski/-ovska*** **(M/F)**
South Balkan		Greek	*Papa-, Mastro-, Archi-, Gero-, Kara-*	*-akis, -atos, -opoulos, -idis, -ides, -iadis, -iades, -ellis, -oudas, -oulis, -as, -eas, -is, -os, -ou*
South Balkan		Albanian		*-aj, -i, -u, -a/-ja*
Two more		Romanian		***-escu***,*-aşcu, -ăscu, -eanu, -anu, -an,- aru, -oru, -anu, -u*
Two more		Hungarian		*-as, -os, -or, -ar, -ász, -ész, -ács, -acz, -szar, -áth, -eth, -y*

Appendix B. Top 10

The following lists were taken from a variety of sources. Some sources are specific in terms of the year the census was taken, but others don't specify a year. The order of names can change slightly from year to year, but that should not matter much. The reader can still get a good idea of some typical names from each nation. Here is the list in alphabetical order by country.

Albania	Hoxha/Hoxhaj, Sheku, Prifti, Çela/Çelaj, Leka/Lekaj, Dervishi, Hysi, Rama, Dibra, Abazi
Belarus	Ivanov, Ivanova, Novik, Zhuk, Moroz, Novikova, Kotova, Petrov, Novikov, Volkova
Belgium	Peeters, Janssens, Maes, Jacobs, Mertens, Willems, Claes, Goossens, Wouters, De Smet
Bosnia	Hodžić, Kovačević, Marković, Petrović, Tomić, Delić, Hadžić, Savić, Halilović, Babić
Bulgaria	Ivanova/Ivanov, Georgieva/Georgiev, Dimitrova/Dimitrov, Petrova/Petrov, Nikolova/Nikolov, Hristova, Stoyanova, Todorova, Hristov, Stoyanov
Croatia	Knežević, Horvat, Kovačević, Pavlović, Blažević, Božić, Lovrić, Babić, Marković, Bošnjak
Czech Republic	Novák/Nováková, Svoboda/Svobodová, Novotný/Novotná, Dvořak/Dvořaková, Černy/Černá, Procházka/Procházková, Kučera/Kučerová, Veselý/Veselá, Horák/Horáková, Krejči
Denmark	Nielsen, Jensen, Hansen, Andersen, Peersen, Christensen, Larsen, Sørensen, Rasmussen, Jørgensen
England	Smith, Jones, Williams, Taylor, Davies, Brown, Wilson, Evans, Thomas, Johnson
Estonia	Tamm, Saar, Sepp, Kask, Mägi, Kukk, Rebane, Koppel, Karu, Ilves

Finland	Korhonen, Virtanen, Mäkinen, Nieminen, Mäkelä, Hämäläinen, Laine, Heikkinen, Koskinen, Järvinen
France	Martin, Bernard, Thomas, Robert, Petit, Dubois, Richard, García, Durand, Moreau
Germany	Müller, Schmidt, Schneider, Fischer, Weber, Meyer, Wagner, Becker, Schultz, Hoffmann
Greece	Papadopoulos, Pappas, Karagiannis, Vlahos/Vlachos, Ioannidis, Economou, Papagiorgiou, Makris, Konstantinidis, Dimopoulos
Hungary	Nagy, Kovács, Tóth, Szabó, Horváth, Varga, Kis, Molnár, Németh, Farkas
Iceland	Blöndahl, Thorarensen, Hansen, Olsen, Anderson, Thoroddsen, Möller, Nielsen, Waage, Bergmann
Ireland	Murphy, Kelly, O'Brien, Ryan, Byrne, O'Connor, Walsh, O'Sullivan, McCarthy, Doyle
Italy	Rossi, Russo, Ferrari, Esposito, Bianchi, Romano, Colombo, Ricci, Marino, Greco
Latvia	Berzina, Ozola, Ivanova, Kalnina, Ozolina, Berziņš, Ozols, Jansone, Ivanovs, Kalniņš
Lithuania	Jankauskienė, Kazlauskienė, Petrauskas, Petrauskienė, Stankevičienė, Jankauskas, Kazlauskas, Stankevičius, Paulauskienė, Vasiliauskienė
Macedonia	Stojanovski, Jovanovska, Jovanovski, Stojanovska, Nikolovska, Nikolovski, Trajkovski, Stojanova, Trajkovska, Ramadani
Netherlands	De Jong, Jansen, De Vries, Van de Berg/Van den Berg/Van der Berg, Van Dijk/Van Dyk, Bakker, Janssen, Visser, Smit, Meijer/Meyer
Norway	Hansen, Johansen, Olsen, Larsen, Andersen, Pedersen, Nilsen, Kristiansen, Jensen, Karlsen

Poland	Nowak, Kowalski/Kowalska, Wiśniewski/Wiśniewska, Wójcik, Kowalczyk, Kamiński/Kamińska, Lewandowski/Lewandowska, Zieliński/Zielińska, Szymański/Szymańska, Woźniak
Portugal	Silva, Santos, Ferreira, Pereira, Costa, Oliveira, Martins, Rodrigues, Sousa, Fernandes
Romania	Popa, Popescu, Pop, Radu, Dumitru, Stan, Stoica, Gheorghe, Matei, Rusu
Russia	Ivanov/Ivanova, Smirnov/Smirnova, Kuznetsov/Kuznetsova, Popov/Popova, Vasiliev/Vasilieva, Petrov/Petrova, Sokolov/Sokolova, Mikhailov/Mikhailova, Fedorov/Fedorova, Morozov/Morozova
Scotland	Smith, Brown, Wilson, Thomas, Stewart, Robertson, Campbell, Anderson, Scott, Taylor
Serbia	Jovanović, Petrović, Nikolić, Marković, Đorđević, Stojanović, Ilić, Stanković, Pavlović, Milošević
Slovakia	Horváth/Horváthová, Kováč/Kováčová, Varga/Vargová, Tóth/Tóthová, Nagy/Nagyová, Baláž/Balážová, Szabó/Szabová, Molnár/Molnárová, Balog/Balogová, Lukáč/Lukáčova
Slovenia	Novak, Horvat, Kovačič, Krajnc, Zupančič, Kovač, Potočnik, Mlakar, Vidmar, Kos
Spain	García, González, López, Sánchez, Gómez, Jimenez, Ruiz, Moreno, Álvarez, Gutierrez, Navarro
Sweden	Andersson, Johansson, Karlsson, Nilsson, Eriksson, Larsson, Olsson, Persson, Svensson, Gustafsson
Ukraine	Melnyk, Shevchenko, Bondarenko, Kovalenko, Boiko, Tkachenko, Kravchenko, Kovalchuk, Koval, Shevchuk
Wales	Jones, Davies, Williams, Evans, Thomas, Roberts, Lewis, Hughes, Morgan, Griffiths

Printed in Great Britain
by Amazon